THE LANGUAGE OF
ADVOCACY

*For Ian, Eddie, Rob and Glen
and all my colleagues at
King's Bench Walk*

THE LANGUAGE
OF ADVOCACY

What to say and how to say it
in the courts of
the English-speaking peoples

by

Keith Evans

BLACKSTONE
PRESS LIMITED

First Published in Great Britain 1998 by Blackstone Press Limited,
Aldine Place, London W12 8AA. Telephone: 0181-740 2277

© Keith Evans, 1998

ISBN: 1 85431 835 7

British Library Cataloguing in Publication Data
A CIP catalogue record for this book is available from the British
Library

Typeset by Style Photosetting Ltd, Mayfield, East Sussex
Printed by Livesey Ltd, Shrewsbury, Shropshire

Contents

About the Author

Keith Evans read law at Cambridge and was called to the Bar by the Middle Temple in 1962. He qualified at the California Bar in 1975. He practised in London for 20 years, for the last seven of them as Head of Chambers, before going to California where he was a professor in an American law school and, at the same time, practised in the California courts. He now divides his time between an American and English practice, and teaches a highly acclaimed seminar on trial advocacy throughout the English-speaking world.

Other books by Keith Evans:

Advocacy in Court and *The Golden Rules of Advocacy*, both published by Blackstone Press, London

The Common Sense Rules of Trial Advocacy, published by West Publishing Co., St Pauls, Minnesota.

Preface

Although English is one of the world's youngest languages, it is more widely used than any language ever has been. And wherever English is spoken, you almost invariably find the Common Law — that system of law which had its beginnings in a rainy little island that was, then, at the top left-hand corner of the known world. From England, the Common Law, with its strange ideas about individual liberty, was carried out to the most distant parts of the planet. Even Scotland, Quebec and Louisiana — all civilian systems owing so much to Roman and French jurisprudence — have their admixture of Common Law, and the most dynamic nation there has ever been, the United States, has 50 separate versions of it.

Transplanted as it has been, the Common Law has inevitably developed in all kinds of different ways; but when you pause to inquire, you recognise at once the overwhelming similarities — everywhere. In particular, the English-speaking trial is recognisably the same animal, from the Antipodes to Alberta. We use much the same language, despite local variations, and common lawyers everywhere all start out anxiously stumbling over their words, searching for the right way of putting it.

The idea for this book came out of an animated conversation between English and American lawyers in a little town in the

Rocky Mountains. Since we all use the same language and start out with the same problems, why not try to draw it all together so as to make it easier for the beginners — for the young brother and sister common lawyers who are going to carry the great traditions into the next millenium?

This is the result. The book has been combed and edited by distinguished lawyers from all over the English-speaking world, and I want to say who they are. In Australia, editing on behalf of the Antipodes, Kate Traill, barrister; in Canada, Daniel W. Hagg, QC, and Chris Fix, barrister and solicitor. In the Commonwealth Caribbean, C. Dennis Morrison, QC, of Dunn, Cox, Orrett & Ashenheim; and in South Africa, Ugo Paladini, Attorney of the High Court. For the subcontinent the editor is Ramni Taneja, who is both an Indian advocate and an English solicitor; and for the Far East, Michael Sherrard QC, who found time to do this during his stint as Master Treasurer of the Middle Temple. Lord McGhie kindly added comments from Scotland; and in the United States, the editing was done by George Heitczman of Pennsylvania who, despite holding the rarest of qualifications, that of a certified patent attorney, prefers to spend most of his time in front of juries.

I want to record my thanks to all of them. It has been the most delightful collaboration, and we all hope that this little book will ease the passage of the newcomer from nervous beginnings to (seemingly) effortless advocacy.

Keith Evans
King's Bench Walk
March 1998

Introduction

Anyone who is really drawn to the idea of becoming a courtroom advocate almost certainly has the capacity to be a good one. Skilled trial advocacy is not, repeat *not*, a mysterious talent that you either have or don't have. Like flying an aircraft, high-quality advocacy is something most people can learn — if they really want to.

This is not to suggest that there aren't natural advocates. The top few per cent in *any* calling have a special talent, and advocacy is no exception. Nor am I suggesting that *anybody* can learn to be a truly competent advocate. You have to have a certain basic fluency in the use of language and you have to have the kind of mind that can learn to think clearly. But if you hadn't had both of these it's unlikely that you'd have been able to pass the qualifying exams in the first place.

In more than 30 years at the Bar — part of the time in England and part of the time in the United States — I can't ever remember encountering an advocate who didn't have all the fluency of language he or she needed - *some* of the time. When fluency fails the average advocate, it almost always fails in the same places. A judge interrupts your argument. How do you deal with the interruption? What words do you use? This is the commonest of situations, yet many advocates get thrown by it. They know their facts and they have the relevant law at their fingertips. If they were talking about the case over a drink in a bar or a pub, they'd be totally fluent. But when interrupted from the bench, they flounder. I floundered for years.

Yet, if they knew the right formula of words to use on such an occasion — and there are half a dozen easy ways of handling the judge's interruption — there would be no floundering at all. By knowing the right words, and by having them instantly available, they would glide smoothly over the interruption, disposing of the problem at the same time as seeming effortlessly in command of the situation.

Another illustration: taking your own witness in what the British and the other jurisdictions call 'in-chief', and the Americans (and, sometimes, the Canadians) call 'direct', is anything but easy. The whole thing ought to sound like a conversation, but with many advocates the exercise sounds stilted and halting. Again, it's mainly a matter of having the right words and the right *form* of question ready to lubricate the interchange between lawyer and witness. Knowing the appropriate words and phrases turns what would otherwise sound like a boring interrogation into an interesting and well-told tale.

In other books, and in seminars, I occasionally touch on these 'appropriate' words and phrases. Again and again, however, I have been asked if there is anywhere a lawyer can go and find them *all* set out, and I always have to admit that I know of no such publication. There are bits here and bits there, scattered through the literature of the law, but I know of no one book — however small — which deals extensively with the language of advocacy as a more or less separate topic. Yet it is worth being treated as a separate topic. The special words and phrases that get you over the hurdles of advocacy are *so* useful, and not knowing them leads to *such* a glaring appearance of incompetence, that a familiarity with this special language ought to be regarded as part of any professional advocate's tool-chest.

This short book is devoted to the language of advocacy used in the courts of the English-speaking peoples — or perhaps I should say the language of advocacy of the English-speaking courts. Either in the text itself or in a footnote there will be set out the variations which apply in most of the different English-speaking jurisdictions, and this text has been edited for such local variations by learned friends from America to Singapore.

The biggest differences, of course, are to be found in the contrast between England and America, and unquestionably, you cannot use the idiom of one in the courts of the other. Formalities are very different. Yet, as I discovered for myself, the useful words and phrases, the endlinks and gadgets, that work in England work equally well in America, and probably in all the other jurisdictions as well. The slightest modification is all that's needed.

The book is divided into two parts. First come the formalities, the correct and incorrect ways of addressing the various tribunals, along with some observations on how first-class advocates handle these formalities. Then come those words and phrases, sentences even, and sometimes short paragraphs, that successfully oil the wheels — how to start and how to finish various tasks in court, how to handle the judge, and so on.

I'm not aiming to be exhaustive: nobody could be. But we *will* touch on all the problem areas and encounter a lot of suggestions as to how difficulties might be handled.

PART ONE

FORMALITIES

1 A Question of Niceness

Before we get to such matters as who gets called 'my Lord' or 'your Honour'[1] and so on, let's spend a little while considering the question of politeness generally. Over this last quarter of a century or so, the judges in America have been complaining more and more bitterly about a falling off in standards of courtesy at the Bar. Indeed, during many years in the English courts, I have noticed a similar trend there. It isn't as pronounced as it can be in America, but an under-current of truculence has occasionally started to make itself felt, and there is a discernible decline in standards or courtesy among some people at the Bar.

Does this matter, and if so, why?

I think it does matter, but my reasons are more practical than philosophical. A trial or an appeal tends to be an intense affair. In civil cases both sides have a big emotional investment in winning. After all, the only civil cases that come to trial are the

---

[1] Footnotes can be the scourge of books that deal with the law, but so as to deal with local variations in different countries footnotes will occasionally be necessary. This one concerns the differences in spelling between English English and American English. Samuel Johnson and Noah Webster have a lot to answer for. Rather than try to appease both camps with clumsy alternatives, the spelling adopted in this book will be English English except in a purely American context.

ones that couldn't be settled. The people involved have adopted
entrenched positions, and 'See you in court' is in many ways like
a declaration of war. Peace initiatives, if any, have failed and
now armour is being buckled on, swords sharpened, the artillery
brought out. This is combat-readiness, and attitudes and emotions
change accordingly.

In circumstances like these it's easy to let aggressiveness creep
in; and once one kind of nastiness takes hold it tends to spawn
other kinds of unpleasantness. Veiled rudenesses, then less veiled
insults start to roughen up the proceedings. Quite soon, the whole
atmosphere, the entire energy, of the courtroom can become
quarrelsome and unkind. I've seen a lot of this, particularly in
America, and it's very counter-productive — for two significant
reasons.

First, it is terribly stressful for the lawyers involved, and the law
is a stressful enough profession without the added discomforts of
quarrelsome days. Apart from anything else, you cannot shake off
this negative energy when you leave court. You take some of it
with you back to chambers or office. You certainly take some of it
home: it affects the rest of your living and bits of it rub off on
those closest to you. And it does you no good at all, physically.

Secondly, if you have a jury, the jurors don't like it. All kinds of
surveys have been carried out to discover how jurors react to all
sorts of things, and there is a remarkable consistency in how they
feel about quarrelsome lawyers. It makes them defensive, cau-
tious, often downright embarrassed. And it makes them less
inclined to listen to what the ill-humoured lawyer has to say.
Since successful advocacy is all about getting your decision-
makers to listen to you *with sympathy*, unpleasantness on the part
of the advocate really strikes at the root of the whole thing. Not
only are you stressing yourself out: at the same time you are
significantly reducing your effectiveness.

The object of advocacy is getting the decision-maker to agree
with you; and since sarcasm, quarrelsomeness and so on tend
to alienate both judge and jury, they are hideously counter-
-productive. Of *course* there are situations where a measure of

forcefulness is called for, and there are times when a rebuke coming from an advocate is well-justified; but such occasions are rare, and your client's interests are far better served if you remember to try to be as nice as you possibly can be all the way through.

This isn't what you see on television: writers and directors have turned the abrasive lawyer into a stock character. And there has always been a style of advocacy that involves the aggressive approach: a lot of lawyers still think it's expected of them. For my own part, after the early, timid years, I found I was becoming somewhat aggressive myself; in one particular case, a difficult one, I actively decided to try a much more gentle approach. The results were astonishing. Hostile witnesses started agreeing that they might indeed have got it wrong. Yes, indeed, the version I was suggesting might well have been the truth of the situation. Everything became surprisingly easier. The judge became, somehow, more human. The jury were wonderfully attentive and came back quickly with the verdict I had suggested they'd feel comfortable with.

Ever since that case I have tried to discipline myself to be gentle, affable even, right the way through — usually with gratifying results. It isn't always easy, being nice, being gentle, in court — it's often far easier to descend into combativeness — but if you can manage it, it brings all kinds of rewards.

I had a woman lawyer come up to me in Cleveland, Ohio, some time ago and ask if I could advise her on how to handle her opponent: 'He is — forgive my language —' she said, 'an asshole' (American English has some very evocative insults) 'and I don't know how to cope. He's nasty, I'm nasty back, the judge is permanently tetchy and the jury obviously feel uncomfortable. Do you have any advice?'

'Try being all sweetness and light,' I suggested. 'Ignore his nastiness, and concentrate on being as nice to him as you possibly can.'

She went away, shaking her head, clearly wondering how unrealistic one could get. Yet a week or so later I got a letter from her: 'He became isolated,' she said. 'I went back to court and did as you suggested. It was difficult but I persevered. I was as nice to him as I could bring myself to be. And the judge got relaxed and so did the jury, and within half a day he was the only nasty guy in the courtroom. The following day *he* started to act all sweetness and light. The trial continues, but it's a much happier experience going to court.'

She hit on something important when she mentioned *relaxation*, because that's what happens when an advocate takes the lead and brings niceness into the proceedings. And when judge and jury are relaxed, when they are not distracted and disturbed by a quarrelsome atmosphere, they focus more intently on the job in hand. They are far more receptive to suggestions coming from a relaxed, pleasant advocate, and if the time comes when a little vehemence and passion creep into his or her presentation, they will be receptive to that too.

When it's a criminal rather than a civil trial, all this is equally true. Aggressiveness and hostility on the part of a prosecutor aren't nearly as effective as niceness; and unpleasantness coming from the defence rarely helps the accused. The clue, all the way through, is to aim to combine relaxation and niceness generally with a fastidious (yet relaxed) politeness to everybody in the proceedings.

One other short point before we come to the actual formalities. As well as aiming to be pleasant and graciously polite, try to be *consistent*. Inconsistency is something your decision-makers will notice immediately. It makes them uncomfortable; but, worse, it makes them mistrustful of you. This is not to suggest that you shouldn't vary your pace and vary your tone, nor indeed that you should never show your teeth — a snarl from an otherwise friendly dog is sometimes effective — but an underlying consistency in your demeanour is important.

Very well. What are these formalities? To start with, who gets called what?

2   Who Gets Called What: the Formal and Informal Ways of Addressing the Judiciary

In America, as in Australia, Singapore, Malaysia and other jurisdictions, *all* judges are addressed as 'your Honour' — when, that is, they are acting in their official capacity. If they are sitting in court, if they are transacting any judicial business in chambers, or if they are away from the court building in order to view the *locus* where something happened, they should always be addressed with formality by everybody involved in the case and should be called 'your Honour'.

In Britain, Canada, India, South Africa and the Commonwealth Carribean, depending on which court the judge is sitting in — and we'll come to a fairly extensive tabulation later — the formal modes of address are 'my Lord', 'my Lady' or 'your Honour', and the same principles apply. When the judge is acting in his or her capacity as judge, *only* the formal modes of address should be used. When one of my opponents in an American trial interrupted what I was saying with the comment 'Say Judge, that's baloney!', his opinion may have been correct but his mode of addressing the bench was not.[2]

---

[2]   This is true throughout most of the English-speaking world, though not in the provincial - as opposed to the federal - courts of Canada. In most of Canada's provincial courts one *can* address the judge in court as 'Judge', or, indeed, as 'Sir', 'Madam' or 'your Honour'.

In most cases in the superior courts of the English-speaking jurisdictions a written record is made: a court reporter is there with his or her stenography machine. (In Britain he or she is still called the 'shorthand writer', and although many of them now operate a machine, pen and ink are still in use.) The 'record' in most English-speaking court proceedings is continuous and complete, and the reason I mention it is simply this: when there is a court reporter/shorthand writer/stenographer present, the judge should always be addressed, and referred to, with complete formality.

In England, proceedings in the judge's chambers are usually conducted *without* a record being made, and the judge can sometimes make such proceedings surprisingly informal. If, as is often the case, the judge is well acquainted with the lawyers involved, he or she may well address them by their first names. This kind of informality should be reciprocated, and the lawyers should *not* address the judge as 'my Lord', 'my Lady' or 'your Honour' but, instead, as 'Judge'. But if the judge kicks off by referring to counsel as 'Mr Hackett' and 'Miss Parker', this lead should be followed and the strictly formal modes of address should be used. Always set out with the intention of using the formalities: ease up on them only when the judge eases up.

When, on the other hand, you meet a judge in the street or restaurant, as a private person not currently and actively engaged in something to do with your case, you don't call him 'your Honour' but 'Judge'. It's the same in America as it is throughout the rest of the English-speaking world. Even though he's 'my Lord' or 'your Honor' when he's acting in his official capacity, if you speak to him on any informal occasion, you call him 'Judge'.[3] In India it is proper to use 'Sir' or 'Madam', but 'Judge' is preferable.

If, on an informal occasion, you are talking to an American *appeal* court judge — a Justice of Appeal — or if you are addressing a British Lord Justice, it is still proper to call him

---

[3]   As in so many other ways, Scotland and Canada are different. 'My Lord' and 'my Lady' are used *both* on formal *and* informal occasions. Informally, a sheriff is addressed as 'Sheriff'.

'Judge'. It's equally proper to call him or her, in America, 'Justice', and, in England, 'Lord Justice' or 'Lady Justice' (in Canada it is 'Madam Justice'); but 'Judge' is shorter and much easier to use in conversation, and no appeal court Justice will ever take offence at being called simply 'Judge'. It's an illustration of the old truism that those who matter don't care, and those who care don't matter. This appears to be true of all the senior appeal judges in all the jurisdictions. In South Africa, *all* judges, whatever their rank, are informally addressed as 'Judge'.

Except in Scotland and Canada, never, ever address a judge, justice or whatever as 'your Honor', 'my Lord' or 'my Lady', when they are *not* acting in their official capacity. I've heard this done in England as well as in America and all it indicates is that the offender is not very aware of the niceties of the profession. Little things like this, however, are usually noticed, and they tend to mark off the true professional from the rest.

The very highest court in the United Kingdom is the House of Lords itself. The Lords hear final appeals from England and Wales, Scotland and Northern Ireland, but they also take cases from places in the Commonwealth. When the Lords act as an appeal court, the members of the court are not randomly chosen from the British aristocracy. They are lawyers, almost all of whom have experience as judges — most of them are former justices of the Court of Appeal or the Scottish Court of Session — and they have been purposely elevated to the peerage so as to sit as members of the 'Judicial Committee' of the House of Lords (or, for the purposes of hearing appeals from certain Commonwealth countries, the 'Judicial Committee of the Privy Council'). If some Duke, Earl or Baron with no legal qualifications tried to barge in and involve himself in the judicial proceedings of the Lords, he would be cold-shouldered and ignored.

The equivalent court in America is the Supreme Court of the United States, and appearing as an advocate in the US Supreme Court is a very different experience from arguing an appeal in the Lords. In the Supreme Court no fewer than nine Justices, in black robes, are ranged from one side of the huge courtroom to the other, sitting behind a great, long wall of raised-up desk, all backed by a vast curtain. In the House of Lords, on the other hand, appeals are heard in a committee room! Five mature gentlemen, dressed in ordinary business suits (no wigs and gowns) hear cases sitting round a rather cramped horseshoe-shaped table - a good example of the way the British, who do so well at fairy-tale parades and pomp and circumstance generally, sometimes play things right down.

How does an advocate address these most distinguished of judges? In the United States Supreme Court they are all 'your Honor': in the House of Lords they are all 'my Lord' — the Lords have yet to get a woman appointed to their Judicial Committee. But what do you call them when you meet them on an *informal* occasion?

As to the US Supreme Court Justices, these nine are the 'senior' lawyers in a country that has over half a million attorneys. Such distinction merits recognition, and the members of the Supreme Court are always addressed, informally, as 'Justice'.

As to the judges in the House of Lords — they are officially known as 'Lords of Appeal in Ordinary' — there has always been some doubt concerning how they should be *informally* addressed by members of the legal profession. It doesn't sound quite right for a lawyer to call a law lord 'Lord Slynn', because that's what a lay person would call him. To settle the matter, some years ago, I asked a couple of law lords how a lawyer should address them informally. They both said they preferred to be called simply 'Judge'. Indeed, this appears to be true of the senior appeal judges in virtually all the English-speaking jurisdictions.

If, of course, a barrister falls into conversation with a law lord *at the Inn of Court of which they are both members*, the correct way to address him is 'Master'. This is because, as a senior judge, the law lord will inevitably have become a 'Master of the Bench' — a 'Bencher' — a member of the governing body of his Inn; and no matter what his rank and station may be in the outside world, when he is actually in his Inn of Court he is regarded as nothing more, or less, than a 'Master'. (Some time back, incidentally, Middle Temple, my original Inn, appointed its first woman Bencher. She was much quizzed — and teased — about whether she should be addressed as 'Mistress'. To this day, however, and despite the strong tides that are now running, she is still addressed and referred to as 'Master'.)

Every common law jurisdiction has a *Chief Justice*.[4] In America, indeed, every state is a separate jurisdiction with its own laws and legislature, its own appeal court structure and its own Supreme Court. There are therefore no fewer than 51 Chief Justices in the United States, and they are all addressed, informally, as 'Chief Justice'. In England, on informal occasions, lawyers and their spouses call the Lord Chief Justice 'Lord Chief'. In Australia the Chief Judge is called just that: 'Chief Judge'.

As I have already said, in America *any* holder of judicial office — and this includes the Federal Magistrate — is addressed, formally, as 'your Honor', and can be properly addressed, informally, as 'Judge'. There is, however, in a number of jurisdictions, a handful of special judgeships where a different kind of informal address is correct. In England, for instance, the head judge of the Chancery Division is known as the 'Vice-Chancellor', and he or she can be addressed informally either as 'Vice-Chancellor' or 'Judge'. In some states in America there are still separate courts of chancery, and the head judges of such courts are usually known as the 'Chancellor'. Lawyers can choose between calling them, on informal occasions, 'Chancellor' or simply 'Judge'.

Additionally, in England, there are the Queen's Bench and Chancery 'Masters', and in the Family Division there are the 'Registrars'.[5] I very much hesitate to describe them as 'minor' judges because of the immense powers they wield and the vast amount of work they handle. They deal, in the main, with all kinds of interlocutory work — what in America is called 'motion practice' — though they also act as judges of first instance in certain matters. In their official capacity the masters are addressed as just that: 'Master'. The Family Division Registrars, in

---

[4]   Except Scotland, which is a mixed common law and civilian system.

[5]   Canada has Queen's Bench Masters, formally addressed as 'Master' or 'Sir'. Australia, too, has Masters — in the Equity and in the Common Law Divisions. Australia also has, uniquely, a judge known as a *Prothonotary*. He is an august version of a Registrar and sits in the Common Law Division of the Supreme Court. On informal occasions he is addressed as 'Mr Prothonotary'.

their official capacity, are addressed as 'Sir' or 'Madam/Ma'am'. If you meet a Master on the street or at a party, you call him simply 'Master'. If you meet a registrar, you have a choice: you can either use 'Sir' or 'Madam', or you can revert to the universal 'Judge'. If you use the latter, rest assured no offence will be taken.[6]

'Your Worship' is an antiquity that seems to be dying out, in England and Wales anyway. Until very recently the police constable who called on the cases in English and Welsh magistrates' courts used to use 'your Worship' all the time, often bellowed in a voice to rival the town crier. It used to reflect one of the differences between barristers and solicitors. The latter always addressed the bench as 'your Worship/s', whereas barristers were schooled to use only 'Sir' or 'Madam/Ma'am'. Many solicitors now use the 'Sir', 'Madam/Ma'am' form of address, and unless the court policeman keeps using 'your Worship', this old appellation won't be around much longer. It still survives in other places around the world, however. In South Africa, it's usual to address the magistrate as 'your Worship' at the outset, but after that to call him or her just 'Sir' or 'Madam/Ma'am'. In Australia, 'your Worship' is still the proper form of address for a magistrate, and on the only occasion when three magistrates sit together — the full Liquor Licensing Court — 'your Worships' is proper. In the Commonwealth Carribean courts there are still *Petty Sessions* courts, where the judges are lay justices — as in England and Wales — and they are addressed as 'your Worships'. There are also some places in India where magistrates are addressed as 'your Worship'. This strange old appellation seems well set to survive into the Third Millenium, whatever happens to it in its original home.[7]

---

[6]   In South Africa even the magistrates have a proper informal mode of address, as far as I am aware the only magistrates in the English-speaking world who do. When they are addressed, not in English but in Afrikaans, the appellation is *Landdross.*

[7]   The Commonwealth Caribbean courts, it must be said, are a fascinating group. The staggeringly high quality of the business-related opinions and judgments that come out of the *Turks and Caicos Islands* impresses any American attorney who reads them, and without The West Indies the Judicial Committee of the Privy Council would have a lot less to do. The list of places encompassed by the Commonwealth Caribbean is a truly romantic roll call: Bahamas, Jamaica, St Kitts & Nevis, Antigua and Barbuda, St Lucia, Dominica, Grenada, St Vincent, Trinidad and Tobago, Guyana and Belize. The Commonwealth Caribbean also includes the British dependent territories of the Turks & Caicos Islands, the British Virgin Islands, Anguilla, and Montserrat.

Let's consider, now, the use of the formal modes of address — your Honour, my Lord and my Lady. They are very easy to use correctly, but unless you know how to handle them it is all too possible to make quite embarrassing mistakes. I actually heard a barrister, once at the Old Bailey, start addressing his judge with the words 'Oh your honourable Lordship' — a positive congeries of error.

Mistakes can be effortlessly avoided if you focus on the grammatical difference between the second person singular and the third person singular of a verb. When you are in ordinary conversation with somebody, you refer to that person as 'you' — second person singular. (Let's ignore the question of whether 'you' is strictly singular or plural: 'thou' has disappeared from modern English, and 'you' now serves, universally, for one or more than one.)

Now, you rarely call a judge 'you' when addressing him or her with formality. It's usually 'your Honour', or 'your Lordship' or 'your Ladyship'. And if you pause to think about it, 'honor', 'lordship' and 'ladyship' are all *nouns,* like your car, your horse, your family — and they are all *third* person singular. The informal question, 'do you see?' therefore translates into 'do*es* your Lordship see?', and the comment, 'you *are* already aware . . .' becomes 'your Honour *is* already aware . . .'. 'I'd invite you to consider . . .' becomes 'I'd invite your Ladyship to consider . . .'.

It's the same with most archaic and formal modes of address — your Majesty, your Holiness, your Excellency, your Grace — and in Spanish and Italian it's still polite to address ordinary people using the third person singular. If you play around with and get thoroughly familiar with this difference between second and third person singular, you'll have no difficulty getting it right in court.

But to continue: most children know that a king or a queen, in film and fiction anyway, is addressed as 'your Majesty', and that a prince or princess is addressed as 'your Highness' — 'Your Majesty, I will obey', 'Your Highness, your wishes are understood'. Similarly, it's 'Your Excellency, I respectfully agree,'

'Your Grace, I have a request,' and 'Your Honour, I appear for the Plaintiff'.

Why, therefore, isn't it 'Your Lordship, I have an application'? One hears it said, now and again, by inexperienced and nervous advocates, but it's wrong. Why, instead, is it *My Lord*, I have an application', or 'During the course of this trial, *my Lord*, we have heard etc.', and *'My Lord*, in this case I appear for the Plaintiff'?

It's an oddity, out of line with the others. The only other formal-language vocatives I can think of that begin with 'my' as opposed to 'your' are 'my Liege' — which in itself is short for 'my liege lord' — and 'my Lady'. The explanation for this is, perhaps, that a lord (or a lady) is a real thing whereas most other formal modes of address are *attributes* — majesty, grace, holiness, honour. But whatever the reason, it needn't concern us so long as the point is made. Whenever the High Court judge is addressed in the *vocative* — 'Oh come on, *darling*, don't get upset', 'I trust, *your Holiness*, that all is well' — you don't use 'your Lordship': you use 'my Lord' or 'my Lady'.

Perhaps it is because 'my Lord' and 'my Lady' refer to real people rather than to polite attributes that these words can very easily be used not just as forms of address, but as the indirect objects in a sentence. For example:

- Usher, would you please hand this exhibit to my Lord?

- Very well, Mr (Witness), tell my Lady what happened then.

This is a proper, and slightly elegant, use of the words. But it would be equally correct, in those examples, to say:

- Usher, would you please hand this exhibit to *his Lordship*?

- Tell *her Ladyship* what happened then.

The choice is yours.

A few more short illustrations, with their correct alternatives, should make all plain:

- May it please your Lordship, this is a running-down action.

- May it please you, my Lord, this is a claim for breach of contract.

- I wonder, my Lord, if we might have a short break at this point: I need to take instructions.

- My Lord, would your Lordship be kind enough to explain to the witness that he must answer the questions and not make speeches?

- Now, Ms (Witness), will you please explain to my Lord and the jury what you did immediately after that?

- Please explain to his Lordship and the jury what you did then.

- Usher, would you please hand this document to my Lord?

- Would you please hand this exhibit to his Lordship?

If, as should be obvious, the judge is a woman — as is more and more frequently the case at the turn of the Millenium — 'my Lord' becomes 'my Lady', and 'your Lordship' becomes 'your Ladyship'.

'Your Honour' causes no such difficulties. 'Your Honour' can be used as a vocative, as a subject and as an indirect object. For example:

- Your Honour, I wonder if your Honour will be rising at the usual time today.

- Does your Honour see page 66 of the exhibit bundle?

- Could you hand this exhibit to her Honour?

- Her Honour will explain the law to you at a later stage in the case.

- Thank you, your Honour.

- I'm much obliged to your Honour.

It's not uncommon, these days, to hear American advocates say such things as 'Ladies and gentlemen, *the judge* will tell you about the law you have to consider at a later stage', or '*Judge Smith* will explain the law to you later in the trial'. Likewise, American advocates often use the vocative 'Judge' instead of 'your Honor' — 'I beg of you, *Judge*, don't make this ruling.'

It isn't proper to use 'Judge' in this way. When the judge is sitting in court (or in chambers, or when on a view — whenever the court reporter is present) the word 'judge' should always be translated into 'his (or her) Honor' or 'your Honor'. I have discussed this matter of style with a lot of American lawyers and judges, and I have argued the point that *custom* tends to change over the years. If it has started to become customary among some lawyers to address the judge in court as 'Judge', shouldn't we accept this as an organic change and live with it? While some of them said 'live with it' and didn't mind at all, on the whole I have had an unequivocal 'No' to this suggestion: it seems that, generally speaking, American judges and experienced advocates alike regret this drift away from formality and very much want to see it stopped.

Although the United States is refreshingly informal when compared with England, America nevertheless has enough formality — usually, anyway, and in certain situations — to accomplish all that formality ought to accomplish. Since this part of the book is all about the formalities of the law court and the advocate, it's worth taking time to consider why *a certain basic level of formality is essential to the successful conduct of business in the courtroom*.

Before coming to this however, let's have a list of who gets called what in various courts. I cannot claim that this list is exhaustive, and changes do occur. If in any doubt, check locally.

'My Lord' or 'My Lady'

House of Lords and Judicial Committee of the Privy Council
Court of Appeal, Scottish Court of Session
High Court of Justice — all divisions
Central Criminal Court at the Old Bailey
(When a High Court Judge sits in *any* Crown Court in England
or Wales, he or she is addressed as 'my Lord' or 'my Lady')
The superior courts of Liverpool and Manchester (some judges
only)
Supreme Courts of the Commonwealth Caribbean
Supreme Court of India
All High Courts of India
The Supreme Court of Appeal of South Africa
South African High Court, provincial and local divisions
South African Circuit Courts
All federal courts in Canada

Your Honor

All judges sitting in the United States, both state and federal,
including the Federal Magistrate

Your Honour

Crown Courts in England and Wales
County courts in England and Wales
(The District Judge in a county court is referred to as 'Sir' or
'Madam/Ma'am')
All judges in Singapore and Malaysia
High Court of Australia
Federal Court of Australia
Family Law Court of Australia
Australian higher state courts, e.g., all divisions of the Su-
preme Court, Court of Appeal, Workers' Compensation Court,
District Courts, county courts, Land and Environment Court
Commonwealth Caribbean magistrates' courts (the equivalent
of the English county courts, presided over by qualified
lawyers)
The South African Black Divorce Court

Indian District Courts, Sessions Courts, Family Courts and City Civil Courts
Certain Indian magistrates' courts

Your Worship

Sometimes used in the magistrates' courts of England and Wales
Commonwealth Caribbean Petty Sessions Courts
Certain Indian magistrates' courts
In Australia, all Local Courts, all Juvenile Courts, Coroner's Court, Liquor Licensing Court, Victim's Compensation Tribunal
In South Africa, the regional or district magistrates' courts (for starting only: thereafter, 'Sir' or 'Madam')

'Sir' or 'Madam/Ma'am'[8]

In England and Wales, magistrates' courts, Juvenile Courts, courts martial, tribunals of all kinds, arbitrations
In India, certain magistrates' courts
In South Africa, regional or district magistrates' courts

Mr President is used in South Africa's Industrial Court and in South African courts martial. In the Constitutional Court, the President may be referred to as 'Mr President'.

Mr Registrar is used to address South Africa's Registrar of Trademarks and Registrar of Patents, and all Australian Registrars.

The *Constitutional Court of South Africa* has issued a *Practice Direction* as to how it wishes to be addressed, introducing a new kind of approach. All Justices of the Court should be addressed as 'Justice X' or 'Justice Y', and *'the expressions "Your Lordship", "Your Ladyship" and similar expressions should not be employed'*.

---

[8] The contraction 'Ma'am' is, apparently, never heard in Canadian courts.

3   Why Formality, Anyway?

We don't need to get too philosophical about this. Just consider a class of excited five-year-olds in the charge of a totally incompetent teacher. If they become unruly — as they are very likely to — nothing will be learned and nothing useful will be accomplished. In all pursuits, there has to be a certain level of order before *anything* can get done. The old-fashioned language of the law court, implying as it does a measure of *deference* to the fact that *one* person — the judge — is in ultimate charge, helps to bring about this necessary level of order. The politenesses of the courtroom serve a tremendously useful function: they make it possible for stressed-out, anxious people to settle their differences without losing their tempers and perhaps their self-control. Without the old-fashioned courtesies it's sometimes difficult not to descend into brawling and quarrelling. And when this happens — as the O.J. Simpson trial demonstrated again and again — everything slows down, everyone involved feels stressed, and — and this is surely the most important part — the chances of arriving at the right result are diminished.

There's also another reason why all our courtroom courtesies are useful. They create an atmosphere, an energy if you like, of something akin to *ceremonial*, and an element of ceremonial is important in a court of law.

The churches know all about ceremonial. So do the armed forces. So do the Native Americans, with their kachinas and dances, and so do peoples in all parts of the world. It is only in this advanced Western civilization of ours that ceremonial has tended to die down, but there's still a lot of it around if you look for it.

Ceremonial has a power of the kind science can't explain — any more than science can explain why Mozart was Mozart and Salieri was Salieri. Reason and clear-thinking don't help us much, not here. Why do a cope and mitre have the impact they do? Why do red tabs on a staff officer's lapel create the kind of energy *they* do? Why have military parades, with bands playing and with every marching man in step, always had more or less the same inspiring, exciting effect on everyone involved? Why are the spectacles of Trooping the Colour or the Changing of the Guard so magnetic to tourists and passers-by?

They are all tapping in to the power created by *ceremonial* — just as the Pope does, and the College of Cardinals, and the village parson, and the Lord Mayors. Without the power generated by the orchestrated ceremonial of the Nuremberg rallies, it's unlikely that Adolf Hitler would have been able to turn Germany into a Nazi state.

There is probably less ceremonial in America than in most places, yet it does exist. The inauguration of the President of the United States is a time when America really bows to, and partakes of, ceremonial; and as many of us know from our own recollection, when a presidential inauguration coincides with a charismatic president, the result can be quite unforgetable — 'Think not what your country can do for you, but what you can do for your country.'

In the courts of California, where it has been my privilege to practise, there resides the awesome power to sentence people to death. There also resides the power occasionally to pronounce verdicts of more than $100 million. There, ordinary citizens sitting on juries sometimes do 'send messages' to which the entire American people pay attention. And most American courts are like this, not just those in California. From a *power* point of view, they are the most potent courtrooms on Earth. Simply in order to handle this power, to control it, they need a certain amount of ceremonial — which necessarily implies a certain level of formality. It doesn't have to be much: the proceedings can be remarkably easy-going so long as that basic level of ceremonial and formality is maintained.

America doesn't go in for the changing-the-guard kind of formalities that still exist in England and elsewhere. Every single session at the Old Bailey starts with three startling bangs of an unseen gavel. The door is thrown open at the far corner of the court and the judge appears on the bench. Some judges sail in with self-important dignity: others scuttle quickly as if shy of the theatrical part they are playing. But as the judge walks from door to chair, the Usher is bellowing the ceremonial incantation:

> All manner of persons having anything to do before my Lords, the Queen's Justices at the Central Criminal Court, draw near and give your attendance! God save the Queen!

It's only slightly less formal in Australia:

> All manner of persons having anything to do before this Honourable Court, draw nigh and you shall be heard. God save the Queen.

America has nothing like this. The usual 'crying onto the bench' in the United States involves no more than:

> Remain seated and come to order. This court, department 47 of the Superior Court of California, Santa Barbara, is now in session, the Honorable James T. Perkins presiding.

. . . And an American citizen, rather like almost everyone else in court, walks onto the bench wearing a black robe over a summerweight suit and flowered tie. 'Good morning folks,' he says as he takes his seat, 'I hope you had a pleasant evening and you're ready for another day of this.'

Although America goes in for comparatively little ceremonial, only a little is needed. But without that basic minimum, the

astonishing power focused in a courtroom can easily reduce the
proceedings to a species of chaos. And this is where we lawyers
come in. This, indeed, is where we can kill two birds with one
stone. If we advocates remember that our polite formalities are
contributing to the *control* of unusual and powerful energies, and
if as a result we learn to be truly courteous, skillfully deferential
and, above all, *nice*, we not only make an essential contribution
to the process of justice, we also score heavily with the decision-
maker. It is worth repeating and emphasising: politeness and
niceness, along with the advocates' adherence to a basic level of
ceremonial, inevitably contribute to the containment and control
of the extraordinary power that infuses the courtroom. They also
make you heard with far greater attentiveness by your decision-
maker — whether judge or jury.

Very well. What next in this section on formalities?

4 Dealing with the Multiple-person Courts

Most appeal courts have two or more judges sitting as a panel. Should you therefore address them in the plural — 'my Lords', 'your Honors', 'Unless your Lordships have any questions, that is how I leave it', 'I hope your Honors will feel that . . .'? The rule used to be that you stuck to the *singular* as much as you could, the theory being that you addressed yourself to the president of the court, the senior judge. This little custom is often observed in England and in South Africa, but it seems to have disappeared from the other jurisdictions.

If you get them interested, the appeal courts talk back at you. Indeed, it's the hallmark of a good performance by the advocate that he or she draws the appeal judges into conversation. Sometimes an appeal court will be fairly unanimous in its thinking. At other times it becomes clear that there is conflict on the bench, and the advocate can find himself the target for questions which are not so much directed at him but at another member of the court: 'I suppose, Mr Monahan, that you would argue (so and so)?' — 'Your Honor, I would indeed.' — 'Well then, Mr Monahan,' (from another judge) 'if that is how you put it, surely you'd run into the difficulty of (such and such)?' Then, before the advocate can answer, the first judge comes back: 'Well, Mr Monahan, you'd no doubt answer that by saying . . .?' Then, from the other one: 'That would surely involve an unjustified interpretation of the case-law!' And so on. Two judges in fundamental disagreement, aiming blows at each other through the advocate standing before them.

How you deal with this depends very much upon the facts and the law of the case, and apart from cautioning you to handle it as politely and tactfully as you can, there's not much general guidance to give you. But it certainly helps if you know the formalities that ought to be employed.

Decide for yourself whether to address the court using the plural or the, now rare, singular, but remember that if you use the singular 'your Honor', or 'my Lord', you should include *all* the judges in your eye-contact. When you are asked a question by one of the judges, look at him or her as you answer, this time addressing the singular 'your Honor' or 'my Lord' to this single member of the court.

When, in addressing an answer to one of the judges, or to the whole bench, you want to refer to something that *one* of their number said, what formal words do you use?

- 'If I may adopt the way her Honor, Justice Sonenschein, put it a little while back, . . .'

- 'I would respectfully use the same reasoning as his Honor, Justice Scalia, . . .'

- 'My Lord, reverting to the question raised by my Lord, Lord Justice Scott, . . .'

So much for the appeal courts. We come now to the opposite end of the spectrum. In England and Wales, an immense amount of work is handled by the *magistrates' courts*, and most of the magistrates are lay persons who do not have legal qualifications. In these magistrates' courts the bench is made up of at least two people and usually three, like most courts of appeal. As in the appeal court, you address the person in the centre, while maintaining as much eye-contact as possible with all of the magistrates. The correct form of address for the magistrate in the centre is 'Sir', 'Madam' or 'Ma'am', and it's proper to start out with the words, 'May it please the Bench'. In argument, you use the words 'Sir' or 'Madam/Ma'am' as you would use 'your Honour' in another court, and if you want to refer to the others on the bench you call them 'your colleagues':

- 'I don't know if you, Sir, and your colleagues, think it would help if you had a view of the *locus*.'

- 'If I may deal, Sir, with the point raised earlier by one of your colleagues . . .'

So much, then, for the multiple-person courts and the problem of addressing them. There follows a strange little chapter, dealing with a centuries-old curiosity which has suddenly sprung into life, bringing with it a problem that has to be solved.

5   The Use of the Word 'Learned'

The word is pronounced, of course, *lear'ned* — learn-ed — and although it is never heard in America, it is still very much part of the formality of the other English-speaking courts. It has two uses.

Whenever you need to refer to some judge who is *not* in your courtroom — as, for instance, a judge mentioned in a law report, or the judge whose decision you are appealing against — what words do you use?

If you are referring to a judge reported in the law reports, you use his title together with his name:

> My Lord, I am seeking to rely upon the judgment of Mr Justice Price in the case of X against Y, reported in the second volume of the All England Law Reports for the year 1997 at page . . .

Once you have identified him by name and title, however, you refer to him thereafter as '*the learned judge*':

> Your lordship will see at page 123, letter B, that the learned judge summarised the position in the following words . . .

When you want to refer to the judge against whose decision you
are appealing, the usual beginning is something like:

> My Lord, this is an appeal from a judgment of Mr Justice
> Kekewich sitting at Birmingham on the 10th of November last
> year. *The learned judge* held that . . .[9]

Whenever, after that, you want to refer to the judge who ruled
against you in the court of first instance, you refer to him as 'the
learned judge', or 'the learned trial judge' or 'the learned judge
in the court below'. You do not refer to him again by name and
title. If you happen to be appealing against a judgment of the
Lord Chief Justice himself — and it is sometimes necessary —
you refer to him during argument as 'the learned Lord Chief
Justice'. Similarly, if it's an appeal against a judgment of the
Master of the Rolls, or of the Vice-Chancellor, or of the President
of the Family Division, you refer to them in argument as 'the
learned Master of the Rolls', or as 'the learned Vice-Chancellor'
or as 'the learned President'. In Britain, it's important to remember all this: if you don't, you will discomfort your court and
brand yourself as someone who doesn't entirely know the ropes.

The other use of the word 'learned' is in referring to your
opponent: 'Your Honour, I appear for the Plaintiff in this case and
the Defendant is represented by my learned friend, Mr Wilmot-
Smith.' If you have as an opponent someone who happens to be
a member of the House of Lords (and although it's not common,
it *can* happen at the Bars of England, Wales, Scotland and
Northern Ireland) then it's both proper and elegant to say: 'My
Lord, in this matter I appear for the Appellant, and the Respon-
dent is represented by my *noble and* learned friend, Lord Irvine.'

In the days before solicitors had the right to appear as advocates
in all courts in Britain, it was only the barristers who referred to
each other as 'my learned friend' — abbreviated, after that first
introduction, to just 'm'friend'. In those courts where solicitors
used to appear as advocates — the county courts and the

---

[9] It is said that counsel once opened, 'My Lord, this is an appeal from a
judgment of Mr Justice Kekewich, but I hasten to assure your Lordship, there *are*
other grounds'.

magistrates' courts were the commonest ones — there was *no* established etiquette as to how they should be referred to by the barristers. The phrases 'my learned friend' and 'my friend' were used by barristers only to refer to other barristers: they tended to refer to solicitor-opponents simply as 'Mr Southgate', or whatever the name was. It's the same in Australia, in those states where they haven't fused the professions.

But times have now changed, solicitor-advocates now have the right to appear in all courts of the kingdom, and there is still, at the time of writing, no established rule as to how a barrister-advocate should refer to a solicitor-opponent and *vice versa*. Whether 'my learned friend' will fall into disuse remains to be seen, just as it remains to be seen whether solicitors and barristers will feel able to perpetuate its use and start referring to each other as 'learned friends'.

It would be a pity, I feel, if the old custom died out. The centuries-old tradition of thinking of and referring to your opponent as a 'friend' is a useful and pleasant one. It started out not as a fiction but as a reality, because the barristers have always constituted a very small profession. (In the 1990s there are still only about 8,500 practising barristers in England and Wales, and in the early 1960s there were fewer than 2,000. They have always been outnumbered, about ten to one, by solicitors.) Thus, because the Bar was so small, because all barristers were members of the extremely collegiate Inns of Court, and because significant numbers of barristers practised 'out on circuit', forming small local Bars in the old assize towns like Cardiff and Swansea, Leeds and Nottingham, there was a real likelihood that barrister-opponents did know each other personally and actually were friends.

Indeed, the Bar worked — and still works — on the assumption that all barristers are acquainted with each other. It's no longer so, of course, but there are still little conventions which perpetuate this presumed universal acquaintanceship. For instance, a barrister who finds that she is opposed by another barrister who is a total stranger, yet whose name she needs to know so as to introduce him formally in court as her opponent, doesn't ever say

'I'm sorry, I don't know your name'. Instead she will say 'I'm sorry, I've *forgotten* your name' — the implication being that since all barristers are friends, she did know her opponent's name at some theoretical time in the past.

Another, somewhat strange, consequence of the Bar's fictitious universal acquaintanceship is that barristers tend not to shake hands with each other. Where this custom originated I cannot discover, though the late Lord Diplock thought he knew. 'Nasty continental habit!' was how he explained it. Other senior lawyers have suggested that the handshake is a demonstration that you are not carrying a weapon, and that there is no need for such assurances between friends. Nobody really knows how the custom began, but it did, in fact, develop something of the power of a taboo: if two English or Welsh barristers, not realising they were both members of the Bar, were introduced and went through the normal business of shaking hands, they were actually embarrassed if they later discovered they'd offended against the old custom. This antique habit, however, whatever one may feel about it, is dying out through most of the English-speaking world.

But returning to the question of whether the phrase 'my learned friend' is likely to survive now that solicitors may appear in courts that were previously the exclusive territory of the barristers, it has to be said that for centuries the barrister was actively discouraged from treating any solicitor as a friend. All barristers are still 'referral lawyers': except in very limited circumstances they don't take clients direct. The client goes first to a solicitor; and if the services of a barrister are required, it is the solicitor who decides which barrister gets the work.

Nowadays, the business of 'rain-making' — finding clients and generating work — is regarded as an essential part of most lawyers' lives. In big partnerships the successful rainmaker tends to be a high earner, and in America there is much TV and other advertising by attorneys. Blatant advertising apart, the picture is not all that different in the rest of the English-speaking world. Gone are the days when lawyers felt it beneath their dignity to let it be known they were available for work.

The English Bar used to be incredibly strict about this. In the book barristers were given at their call — Boulton's *Conduct and Etiquette at the Bar* — there appeared a section entitled 'touting, advertising and publicity', and the message was, for barristers, 'none of the above in any circumstances'. From pupillage onward, the barrister was conditioned to regard it as slightly worse than incest even to hint that he was available to take a case. It was seriously frowned on for a barrister to have a business card. If he chanced to meet a solicitor at a social gathering, it was regarded as utterly improper for him to discuss anything to do with the law. If he appeared on radio or television he had to be described only as 'a barrister': if he let his name be used in any circumstance which could conceivably be regarded as self-publicising, he risked being disbarred. It was as bad as that.

Although much has changed in the last twenty years, such that many barristers' chambers now circulate brochures giving profiles of their membership, old habits die hard and there are still many barristers who grew up under the old conditioning. We were positively commanded not to include solicitors among our friends; and although most of us, no doubt, made exceptions, those exceptions were few and far between. The younger end of the Bar doesn't hold firmly to this old taboo, and the rules have in any case been relaxed. But it is against this centuries-old background that the question has to be considered of whether the phrase 'my learned friend' is headed for the museum or not.

I, personally, hope it remains. Despite the brain-washing I had as a barrister, and despite my quick acceptance that 'touting, advertising and publicity' was a frightful thing, I nevertheless had a few good friends who were solicitors, and one of them was a first class advocate. I would have been very happy — still would be, indeed — to refer to him as 'my learned friend'.

Solicitors who do a lot of advocacy have always been as good at the job as most barristers. They have to pass a final exam at least as challenging as the barristers', and those comparatively few solicitors who are going to appear in the higher courts will all have undertaken extra studies in advocacy. They will be 'learned' in every sense that the barrister is 'learned', despite not having eaten dinners at an Inn of Court. The question, therefore, is whether the barristers will be prepared to call a solicitor 'friend'. I well understand how inhibited some people are going to feel about this, yet what does 'niceness' require in these circumstances?

A few years down the road and we'll know the answer to this one. Perhaps the simplest approach would be to adopt the style of the Commonwealth Caribbean courts. There, the professions have been fused, and any professional opponent you have in court is referred to as 'my learned friend'. Certainly, I hope that an elegant and pleasant old phrase (and concept) isn't consigned to oblivion by narrow-mindedness on the part of a distinguished profession.

But let's get back to the formalities.

6 Putting Your Case

This is a formality which does *not* apply in America; but in England and Wales, Australia, the Commonwealth Caribbean, India, Singapore, Malaysia and, it seems, in all the other English-speaking jurisdictions, it's essential for all advocates to understand exactly what it requires and to be scrupulous about putting it into operation. What it amounts to is this.

Because of the way the 'adversary system' works in an English-speaking trial, the party who brings the case almost invariably has the burden of proving it. Thus, the prosecution or the plaintiff's side almost inevitably go first. They explain their case in an 'opening speech' or 'opening statement'; then they call their witnesses and take them through their evidence,[10] thus exposing them to cross-examination; they prove their documents and other exhibits; and when they have done all they can, they tell the court that they 'close' their case. In America they say they 'rest' their case — 'The Plaintiff rests, your Honor'. In England and most other jurisdictions one usually hears it put slightly differently: 'My Lord, that is the case for the Crown', or 'That is the case for the Plaintiff, your Honour'.

---

[10] In America, it would be 'take them through their *testimony*'. The Americans make the distinction between *testimony*, which is what the witnesses say on oath, and *evidence*, which refers to documents and other exhibits.

At that stage, the defending lawyers will sometimes argue that the plaintiff (or the prosecutor) has failed to make out a case that has to be answered. If the judge agrees, that's the end of it and judgment will be entered accordingly. If the judge doesn't agree then the defence usually call witnesses of their own and 'put on' the case for the defence. Then come the 'final submissions' or 'final speeches' from both sides — known in America as 'closing argument' — and, if it's a jury trial, the judge 'sums up' the evidence and directs the jury as to what law they must apply. If it's a non-jury case — a 'bench-trial' — this summing up is, of course, omitted.

The important, if obvious, point is that the case for the accusing party and the case for the defending party are *successive*: one follows the other. And this is where the formality, the rule indeed, about putting your case comes into play.

The defending advocate is *presumed* to know what witnesses he or she has available, and he or she is also presumed to know what those witnesses are likely to say. In England and Wales, and in most other jurisdictions, it is normal to have among one's papers *signed* statements from all one's own witnesses. Sitting there in court, listening to the witnesses for the other side, the defending advocate is *presumed* to be able to identify, instantly, how the account given by these opposing witnesses is in conflict with the account his or her witnesses will be giving when the time comes. When, therefore, he cross-examines these adverse witnesses *it is his duty* to ask them about all such conflicts. He *must* give the adverse witness the opportunity of commenting on (and in most cases, denying) the version of events the defence's own witness or witnesses will be giving when they get their chance.

There are no strict rules as to how exactly this should be done, and there are no rigid rules as to what words should be used. One usually hears defending counsel use the time-hallowed phrase, 'I put it to you that . . .' (then giving his own witness's version), but any form of words will do, so long as they clearly stake out the conflict and give the witness the opportunity of dealing with it. For example:

Q: You have told my Lord that you inspected the machine on the morning of the accident. Is that correct?

A: Yes.

Q: And you said that you noticed the machine guard was in place?

A: Yes, I did.

Q: I have to suggest to you that's not correct.

A: Oh, yes it is.

Q: I must put it to you that when you inspected the machine that morning, you saw that the guard had been partially removed and pushed away from the cutting surfaces?

A: No.

Q: And you told Mr Singh you would get an engineer to re-instal the guard.

A: No, that's not right.

Q: And you told him, didn't you, that he should carry on using the machine, but to be careful?

A: No, that's not true.

Q: Let's turn now to the question of what other workers were present when you made your inspection. You do agree, do you, that there *were* bystanders at that time? . . . etc.

Another illustration. Here, the advocate is cross-examining the police officer who arrested his client and charged him with driving while impaired by alcohol. He is sometimes 'challenging' the testimony the policeman has already given, sometimes trying to pick up advantage-points as he goes along, but always 'putting' the version his client will give when his turn comes. It's the advocate's bounden duty to do this, even though it can sometimes lead to calamitous results:

Q: You said that the car driven by the Accused was weaving from side to side.

A: Yes, Sir.

Q: That's not correct, is it?

A: Yes it is, Sir.

Q: And you say that as he came into Berkeley Square, his car mounted the kerb?

A: Yes, Sir, it did.

Q: I'm sorry to have to suggest it, Officer, but you are making that up, aren't you?

A: Certainly not, Sir.

Q: The time came when you pulled in front of him?

A: Yes, Sir.

Q: And signalled him to stop?

A: Yes, Sir.

Q: He did stop, didn't he?

A: Yes, Sir.

Q: Positioning his car correctly at the kerbside?

A: Yes, Sir.

Q: Did you then go up to his driver's window?

A: Yes, Sir.

Q: And motioned him to wind it down?

A: Yes, Sir.

Q: Which he did?

A: He did indeed, Sir.

Q: And you asked him to get out of his car?

A: Yes, Sir.

Q: Which, again, he did?

A: Yes, Sir.

Q: You say, at that point, he was swaying on his feet. I put it to you that you are making that up as well?

A: No, Sir, I'm not. He was swaying on his feet, his eyes were glazed and his breath was smelling of drink, Sir.

Q: And, then, you asked him to get into the back of the police car. Is that correct?

A: That's correct, Sir.

Q: And he did get in?

A: Yes, Sir.

Q: And he found himself sitting next to a large lady wearing a fur coat?

A: No, Sir. That was police dog 'Charlie'.

It's one of the low experiences of the advocate, a cross we all have to bear, that the client's version isn't always entirely accurate.

Let me repeat, and emphasize, that you don't have to use any formal words when putting your case. As long as you make it absolutely clear what your version is, and give the adverse witness a fair opportunity of dealing with it, you are doing it correctly. Indeed, the phrase 'I put it to you that . . .' can sound awfully pompous: it's purest 'lawyer language', and most first-class advocates make a point of avoiding 'legalese' as much as they can.

If you *don't* put your case as you should, it will be *presumed* that you didn't have a conflicting version to put. When, therefore, your client and your other witnesses start giving their conflicting version, it will be *presumed* that they are making it up as they go along. The judge will intervene with the accusing words, 'That wasn't put'. Your opponent will make the same comment. At that point your witness loses all credibility in the judge's eyes. If the judge alone is the tryer of fact, he will almost certainly dismiss this part of the evidence as worthless. If he is sitting with a jury, he will make a point of telling them that your witness's version 'wasn't put' and explain how this reduces its credibility.

Think how you would feel if this happened to you. You have your witness statements in writing; you also have, in writing, exactly what your client is going to say. Yet through your forgetfulness or unawareness you fail to 'challenge' opposing witnesses by putting your own witnesses' version — and, as a result, your witnesses are disbelieved.

The only way out of this grievous situation is to ask for a break. If the material you failed to put *was* in a written statement, ask the judge to give you a moment to speak to your opponent. Show your opponent the passage in the statement and tell him, straight, that you forgot to put it. An honest opponent will accept the position, and between you this can be made clear to the judge. Be prepared to eat large quantities of humble pie. An abject apology for your incompetence should get you out of trouble.

But it looks terribly unprofessional. If you *had* put your case properly, and challenged those parts of the evidence you should have challenged, your opponent might have dealt with his case quite differently. Trying to squirm your way out of trouble in this way is as undignified and unfair as asking to have back your last half-dozen moves in a game of chess. Neither your judge nor your opponent is likely ever to forget it. So take infinite care to make sure you understand, and always comply with, this most demanding of formalities.

7 Objections

We come now to a truly American problem from which other English-speaking advocates are comparatively free — the almost military formality of the American objection. Objections in most other English-speaking courts can sometimes be very languid affairs in comparison. The advocate hears some potentially objectionable evidence creeping in, so he slowly gets to his feet:

'My Lord.'

'Yes, Mr Hopkins?' asks the judge. Opposing counsel sits down immediately, instantly yielding the forum.[11] Hopkins casually adjusts his gown about his shoulders.

'My Lord . . .' He pauses, reaching behind his shoulder and adjusting the pigtails of his wig. (The antique uniform has practical uses now and then, and gives one a moment to get callibrated, to think up some arguable justification for keeping the evidence out.)

---

[11] This is a courtesy which exists throughout the English-speaking world. If your opponent stands up in the middle of something you are doing, sit down at once and give him the floor. This, incidentally, can be an effective tactic for dealing with a troublesome opponent, one who interrupts with comments from a seated position. The moment he barges in with *any* comment, sit down. He won't carry on for long.

Hopkins plays for a little more thinking-time: 'My Lord, my friend surely doesn't want to ask that question?'

'Oh,' inquires the judge. 'Why not?'

'Well, my Lord, it er . . ., it er . . .' — more adjusting the gown — 'er . . . it would involve the witness giving hearsay evidence, my Lord.'

'Yes, I see,' says the judge, and turns to other counsel. 'That's bound to be right, isn't it, Mr Murphy?'

Addressed by the judge, opposing counsel immediately rises to his feet. 'Well, my Lord, if m'friend doesn't *like* my question, I'll try it another way — if it please your Lordship.'

'Yes, very well,' says the judge. 'Do let's get on.'

In England and Wales, it's almost as if it is felt to be slightly impolite to interrupt one's opponent with an objection — rather unfriendly, indeed. Unless there's some unpleasantness which has developed between counsel, objections are not all that common, they are not often made in an obstructive manner, and they are very rarely aggressive. In other jurisdictions, Australia for instance, there is no sense that an objection might be seen as an impoliteness: 'I object to the question on the ground of lack of relevance,' is a perfectly courteous intrusion. It's the same in Canada and in most other places.

In the American courts, on the other hand, the making of an objection is both complicated and demanding. We are brought back, here, to the 'record' — the virtually verbatim record of *everything* that is said and done during trial. If a matter goes to appeal, the appeal court will have strict regard to that record. In particular, if anything has been 'stricken from the record', for purposes of appeal it will be disregarded. Furthermore, if the record doesn't show that there was an *immediate* objection to whatever is complained about, the appeal court will disregard the objection. It will be treated as having been *waived*.

Just as other English-speaking advocates have the duty to 'put their case', so the Americans have an equally demanding duty to get their 'timely objection' on the record. Otherwise they can't complain later that something was inadmissible.

Understandably, this changes the atmosphere of the whole trial. It means that one has to be constantly on the look-out for anything inadmissible, ready with an appropriate objection. And 'appropriate', in this context, means that you have to be ready to tack onto the word 'Objection!' a succinct — and instantaneous — justification for why you are objecting:

'Objection, your Honor. Calls for hearsay.'

'Objection, your Honor. Best evidence rule.'

'Objection, your Honor. This testimony is cumulative.'

You have to be constantly on your toes, ready with an objection that is immediate and specifically justifiable — as ready, indeed, as someone who is clay-pigeon shooting, or 'shooting skeet' as it is called in America.

Because the rest of us don't have this instant need to protect the position for appeal, and because we work on the (usually justifiable) assumption that our opponent is going to stick to the rules — as much on a point of honour as anything else — we can afford to be just a little relaxed, in a way no American could be. Of *course* it changes the energy of the courtroom, and in America it undoubtedly provides the soil in which hostility and aggressiveness between the lawyers can take root. After all, if the lawyers are sitting there, obliged by the system to have their hands close to their gun-belts, it's perhaps not surprising if there's the occasional shoot-out.

In the early 1970s, at a time when I had never been into an American courtroom, I was invited by a judge to sit in on one of his cases. We met in his chambers shortly before the case began, and he briefed me on what to expect. One thing he said stuck in my mind: 'Counsel in the case,' he told me, 'are both inexperienced. The prosecutor is a very young Assistant DA and on the other side is a brand new Public Defender. So therefore,' he said with a wry smile, 'we can expect the objections *to be flying thick and fast.*'

And he was right. Both young advocates kept up a constant barrage of objections all the way through, until eventually it seemed as if this was the main purpose of the proceedings — to find fault with the opponent, to wrong-foot him wherever possible, to interrupt incessantly. As they lurched through the afternoon, becoming more and more familiar with being on their feet in court, they both got more and more aggressive with each other. By the end of the day, they were hardly on speaking terms, and it was clear that they both thought they were doing what was expected of them. Everyone in court, except the two combatants, was quite drained. There's no doubt about it: the American objection, unless really understood by the lawyers involved, and unless used with wisdom and discretion, encourages combativeness. And this can quickly deteriorate into the kind of nastiness I was referring to earlier.

Although it isn't directly connected with the formality of objecting, there's another factor which contributes to the hostile energies in so many American courtrooms; and although this involves a short diversion, I feel it ought to be dealt with. It concerns politics.

In many ways, America is a far more vigorous democracy than exists elsewhere. Holders of public office are almost invariably *elected* into the positions they hold, and this can include everybody from the members of the local school board to the state's Chief Justice. Many states elect their judiciary just as they elect their congressional representatives, and there is one office-holder in particular who carries much of the responsibility for the aggressiveness of the American courtroom. This is the District Attorney.

The position of District Attorney — the head of a locality's prosecuting department — has been regarded, for generations now, as a stepping-stone to higher political office; and an ambitious politician who can get himself or herself elected as the

Attorney-General of a state is well placed to become that state's next governor. Indeed, President Clinton himself clearly illustrates the way these rungs on the political ladder can be climbed.

Accordingly, American history is studded with examples of the crusading District Attorney, the DA who promises the electorate that he will eradicate this or that kind of behaviour in his locality. He sets himself up as a kind of law-and-order champion, promising to rid his community of organised crime, or corruption, or prostitution, or gang warfare, or drug traffickers, or whatever seems to be bothering the electorate most.

And he has to deliver on his promises, otherwise he risks being turned out of office at the next election. While he is in office, therefore, there is a tendency for his prosecuting department to be geared to his political advancement. When significant prosecutions are brought, the DA and his assistants strive mightily to get a conviction. There is little of the detachment of the English prosecutor: these prosecutors are dedicated and committed, and trials have often been used to show-case for the electorate what a thrustful, tough-on-crime, effective District Attorney they have. If you ever get the chance of seeing the newsreels of the *Hauptmann* trial, during the 1930s, you'll see this process at its ugliest. The baby of the aviator Charles Lindberg, one of America's greatest celebrities of the time, had been kidnapped, and there was an understandable outcry, demanding that the kidnapper be found and punished.

The trial of Hauptmann was positively gladiatorial, and the impression one gets, throughout, is that it was much more important to get a conviction than to ensure a right result. Hauptmann was convicted in the end, and he died in the electric chair; but doubt has lingered, over the years, as to whether or not this was an appalling miscarriage of justice. Watching the vehement performance of the prosecutor, and taking in the lynch-mob atmosphere of the whole proceedings, one is bound to be disquieted. Is *this* how a trial ought to be conducted? And is it indeed *possible* to bring niceness, detachment, courtesy and a balanced sense of professional fair-play into courtrooms that are so often used as political hustings?

Whatever the answer to such a vexed question, the American trial-lawyer has no choice but to learn when and how to object — how to make his or her objections in such a way as not to reduce the proceedings to a combat zone, and *how to do it in such a way as not to interfere with the effectiveness of his or her advocacy.* Hold fast to this last point and much will take care of itself. Remember that every time you object, you risk having your jurors wonder what you are trying to conceal from them. Remember how easy it is to devolve into the appearance of combativeness and into combativeness itself. Remember how objections inevitably interrupt the flow of the proceedings; and remember, too, that over-objecting is the sure mark of an inexperienced attorney.

When you object, *try to do it as dispassionately as you can.* Never sound triumphant. Never sound impatient or aggressive. And never, by any flicker of expression on your face, or by any other body language, reveal your feelings when the judge rules on your objection. Some advocates engage in a little pantomime when their objections get turned down. They look at the jury and roll their eyes in a show of disbelief, or throw down their pen in disgust. Some even complain, audibly, to their co-counsel. Quite apart from the fact that this kind of behaviour is desperately unprofessional, it never achieves anything positive with a jury. As I've already said, many surveys have been conducted as to how jurors respond to various aspects of the trial process, and over and over again they say, first, that there were far too many objections, and, secondly, that they took against lawyers who couldn't accept an adverse ruling with good grace.

A poker-face is what's needed. Make your objection as quietly as is consistent with its being heard clearly, state your ground for objecting as succinctly and dispassionately as you can, and receive your judge's ruling in bland contentment. In most American courts you can make your objection from a seated position, and you may think it is better to do it seated, since this reduces its apparent intrusiveness. If you try to be slightly *casual* in all your objections, you'll avoid most of the pitfalls.

But do you know your Evidence Code and case law well enough to be able to make a snap judgment on whether you need to object? Could you, with an appearance of casualness and effort-lessness, assign a succinct reason for your objection, there and then? It's by no means easy, and there are few opportunities for practice. What follows, therefore, is a list of the commonest objections, with the briefest of 'justifications' to accompany them.

I do not intend, incidentally, to try to enlighten anybody on the law of evidence, or on the law of civil or criminal procedure. A proper knowledge of these is an essential part of the advocate's stock in trade, and there are many good books, both short and long, which deal with evidence and procedure. One of the most useful guides as to when, why and how to make an objection is a book by Ed Heafey of Crosby Heafey Roach & May, called *California Trial Objections,* published by California's Continuing Education of the Bar. It's an inquiry into the rules of evidence which underlie all proper objections, and despite its title it is usable in all the states. But it also summarises things *so* clearly that it offers really practical help in the heat of the moment. All I aim to do here is to set out, with brief comment, those objections that are most likely to be needed or encountered.

First, let's be clear about what, exactly, *can* be objected to. It isn't only questions: it's anything that looks as if it is going to mislead, or going to cause the breach of a rule of some kind. There are six categories of proper objections, as follows:

1. *THE 'MEAT' OF THE QUESTION* For example, the question may call for hearsay. It may call for information which is privileged, or irrelevant, or immaterial. It may call for a 'narrative answer', or it may invite an opinion from a witness who hasn't been qualified as an expert. It may call for 'speculation' by the witness. There is also a thing called the 'argumentative' question, and it could fit into either this or the next category.

2. *THE FORM OF THE QUESTION* It may be a leading question, containing its own answer, or it may be 'compound' — two or more questions rolled into one. It may be a question that 'assumes facts not in evidence' a hypothetical question which is not declared to be hypothetical. A question may be

'vague', or 'ambiguous', or 'overbroad' or even 'unintelli-gible'. All these invite permissible objections in America. (Indeed, when you have thoroughly familiarised yourself with the 'meat' objections and the 'form' objections, you are well-equipped. There aren't too many more, all told.)

3. *THE WAY YOUR OPPONENT DEALS WITH FORMALITIES* For example: the 'best evidence rule' requires that the originals of documents should be produced unless their absence is satisfac-torily accounted for. Although the Federal Rules are very easy-going on this, allowing photocopies of just about anything unless there is a dispute as to authenticity, some states still have much stricter best evidence rules. If, therefore, there is doubt as to the genuineness of any particular document, and your opponent is trying to get by using a copy, it is imperative to make the objection and put him to strict proof.

Another illustration: in America, there is a firm rule which says you may not get a witness to say *what* she perceived until you have 'laid a foundation', i.e. until you have got her to explain *how* she was able to perceive it. You can't, for instance, ask a witness about the colour of traffic lights until you have had her tell the court that she was in a position to see them, and *did* in fact see them. It's an example of the way America sometimes demands almost military precision in its courts, and an advocate has to be meticulous in following this rule. Any failure to 'lay a proper foundation' is likely to attract an objection, and if — as is the case with some advocates — you just don't understand the rule, you can be reduced to a state of paralysis by such objections.

In this category there is also the 'parole evidence rule', the rule (with its various exceptions) which says that you cannot get a witness to testify in such a way as to add to or detract from a contract that has been reduced to writing. If your opponent breaches this rule, you are entitled to object.

4. *MISQUOTING THE EVIDENCE* A close cousin of 'misquoting' is 'mischaracterizing' the evidence, and either can be objec-ted to. But be aware that, here, you are moving from

concrete, strictly knowable fact — misquoting — into the realm of opinion and literary criticism — mischaracterizing. Sometimes it will be obvious that your opponent is inviting the decision-maker to put a strained construction on the facts, but except in extreme instances it's bound to be question of judgment. Is she mischaracterizing the evidence? Surely, that's a question for the decision-maker to answer. This is an objection to be used only with considerable caution.

5. *THE 'UNRESPONSIVE' ANSWER* The answer may be 'non-responsive'. Instead of answering the question the witness may start making a speech. Worse, he might blurt out something blisteringly inadmissible, something that really affects the case. If this happens, you may need a new trial. You certainly need to make sure the appeal court will give consideration to the matter, and this means that you have to put an immediate objection on the record.

This objection is in a category of its own, *because it is the advocate examining the witness who lodges it.* All other objections are, effectively, criticisms of the advocate who is on his or her feet: this one is a criticism of the witness, and it is the advocate on his or her feet who makes it.

When I first heard this objection used properly I was struck by the businesslike elegance with which it was done. This, more or less, is how it went:

The advocate asked a question and the witness started to make a speech. As soon as it was clear this was happening, the advocate held up his hand in a stop-sign gesture and and broke in on the witness with the words, 'Please excuse me, Mr [Witness]'. Then, immediately turning to the bench:

> Your Honor, would your Honor be good enough to *direct* the witness that his answers must be responsive to the question? [Then he carried straight on, without a pause:] And, your Honor — move to strike all the words after [so and so].

The judge complied, as most judges will, and on went the questioning. When the witness did it again, the advocate gestured again with his hand:

> Forgive me again, Mr [Witness]. Your Honor, would your Honor *admonish* the witness that he must answer the question put? And, your Honor — move to strike all the words after [so and so].

He did it every time the witness gave him cause to. He dropped the bit about asking the judge to admonish the witness and simply said, 'Move to strike all the words after [so and so]', or 'Move to strike the whole answer as being non-responsive'. And the judge so ordered every time.

If the advocate forgets to do this — and many do — there, on the record, remains the offensive answer; and because there was no 'timely objection', the appeal court won't concern itself with the issue of whether what came out was admissible or not. It came in, it wasn't objected to and it's now an integral part of the record. Take great care with this. As a formality it's a very important one.

(Notice, incidentally, one small detail: when the advocate 'moved to strike' the unresponsive answers, he didn't say '*I* move to strike', but simply 'Move to strike'. Dropping the pronoun, in this phrase, is American idiom and it's quite proper.)

6. *THE 'RAG-BAG' CATEGORY*   This includes the following:

- Your opponent is over-egging the pudding, i.e. calling more and more witnesses to prove the same thing again and again. This is referred to as 'cumulative evidence' and the judge has a *discretion* to cut it off.

- Your opponent keeps asking the same question, repeatedly, even though he or she has received an answer. Some English barristers are dreadful offenders in this, and in all jurisdictions it can be formally objected to. Again, it's in the discretion of the judge whether he stops it or not.

- Your opponent is trying to 'impeach' your witness, i.e. trying to demonstrate that he or she is unreliable, but isn't doing it properly. If you want to undermine a witness by demonstrating that he has made a 'prior inconsistent statement' — and this may include a witness you yourself have called if that witness is ruled to be 'hostile' — you have to show him the prior inconsistent statement and give him the opportunity of commenting on it before you can have the statement admitted into evidence.[12] There is also a rule that you can't try to impeach one witness with another witness's statement. If your opponent isn't following these rules you can object on the ground of 'improper impeachment'.

- When your witness has been cross-examined, you may decide to ask some further questions. (In America this is called 're-direct examination': in other jurisdictions it's known simply as 're-examination'.) If you 're-examine', you *must* confine yourself to matters that were dealt with during your opponent's cross-examination. Certainly it is possible, with the judge's permission, to ask questions outside the scope of cross-examination, but the judge might not grant leave, and it gives a very poor impression of unprofessionalism on your part if you have to make the request. If, therefore, you start asking questions on matters that weren't dealt with in cross-examination, you are likely to attract an objection.

- In some states, there is also a rather curious rule which says you must confine your *cross-examination* to matters which were dealt with during direct examination. But there are several exceptions to this rule, it's all within the judge's discretion anyway, and I suggest you make local inquiry.

I don't claim to have caught them all, but if you become thoroughly familiar with the objections discussed here, you should have no difficulty in court. Let's end this chapter with a list, setting out the actual words that may properly be used to

---

[12] Known as the *Rule in Queen Caroline's Case*. It is also set out in the Federal Rules, Rule 613(a).

make objection. Note that you don't have to make some sort of speech, and that an *extremely* brief reason for your objection is all you need. Some judges won't tolerate anything more. As pointed out earlier, you can do it seated, and it ought to be done quite quietly and without drama. You can always begin with 'Objection, your Honor, . . .' then add one of the following, verbatim:

THE 'MEAT' CATEGORY
  'Calls for hearsay'
  'Irrelevant'
  'Immaterial'
  'Argumentative'
  'Calls for speculation'
  'Calls for a narrative answer'
  'Calls for an opinion from a non-expert witness'
  'Calls for privileged information'

THE 'FORM' CATEGORY

  'Leading'
  'The question is compound'
  'The question assumes facts not in evidence'
  'The question is vague'
  'The question is overbroad'
  'The question is ambiguous'
  'The question is, I'm afraid, unintelligible'

(As to these last, one can combine them: 'The question is overbroad, ambiguous and vague.' But take care. You don't want to sound combative.)

THE 'FORMALITIES' CATEGORY

  'Offends against the best evidence rule'
  'Offends against the parole evidence rule'
  'Lacks foundation'

THE 'MISQUOTING' CATEGORY

  'Counsel is misquoting the testimony'
  'Counsel is mischaracterizing the testimony'

THE 'UNRESPONSIVE ANSWER' CATEGORY

This has already been dealt with in detail at pp. 51–2.

THE 'RAG-BAG' CATEGORY

'This evidence is cumulative'
'The question has been asked and answered'
'This is improper impeachment'
'Doesn't arise out of cross-examination'

One last thing, before we leave the business of the American objection. It concerns a fairly fundamental difference between the British and the American way of doing things, and I unhesitatingly declare that, in this instance, I much prefer the American way. In England, and in some other jurisdictions, the judge intervenes in the proceedings far, far more than ever happens in America. Although English *advocates* don't go in for all that many objections, some *judges* are notorious for the way they interfere, and you are far more likely to get an objection coming from the bench than from your opponent.

In America, on the other hand, the judge waits for your opponent to object and, if no objection is made, he lets it go — though American judges sometimes send signals that they are *expecting* an objection, with raised eyebrows, a hard expectant stare or other body language; but they don't intervene. We are supposed to be operating to the adversary system on both sides of the Atlantic; and just as the Americans can take a lesson from the British in how to maintain an easy-going formality, so the British, along with a lot of the other English-speaking judiciary, could learn much about impartiality, and the appearance of impartiality, from the Americans.

Before embarking on the next section of this book, let's pause and consider what we actually mean by the 'Language of Advocacy'.

8   What Do We Really Mean by the 'Language of Advocacy?'

We normally think of *language* in its usual sense — a spoken or written assemblage of words, grammar and syntax that can be used to communicate messages; messages involving commands or comments, feelings or ideas. But it goes further than that.

Studies have been done by psychologists to find out how exactly 'messages' are conveyed, and they have come up with some interesting — not to say alarming — results. They have discovered, for example, that *words play only a small part in communication.*

Shocking, isn't it? Much more important than the actual words used is *tone of voice*. This, so the tests show, is the carrier for over a third of the message. The words themselves convey only between 7 and 10 per cent; and as to the rest — nearly two thirds of the whole — *this* is communicated by the *body-language* of the speaker.

I found that rather troubling when I first heard it. I am more used to it now, especially after reading about the studies that proved it. But I experimented with it as well. I suspended my disbelief and made the intellectual assumption that it was right — 60 per cent body-language, 30 per cent tone of voice, 10 per cent actual words spoken — and I tried to prepare my next case, remembering that those percentages might be valid and not some crazy psychologist's invention.

Tone of voice I knew something about: I was very used to my voice in court; I knew I varied my pace and, very importantly, I knew when I was speaking loudly enough to be heard. But I made a conscious decision to listen out for 'tone of voice' and to bear in mind that alleged 30 per cent.

Body language was different, a slightly *outré* concept, and an unfamiliar one. Nevertheless, I noticed quite soon that I had been using body language all my life — not just in the courtroom — and I'd never really given it a thought. Nobody mentioned it when I was a student. I never heard talk of it at the Bar, either in England or America. Body language was something, or so I thought, that was explored by articles in teenage magazines. But as soon as one thinks about it seriously, one begins to see that, yes indeed, it's bound to be a carrier of information — and a fairly important one at that. To be more exact, body language is bound to convey an *impression* to the listener/viewer. It's how the listener/viewer *responds* that matters — but that response is bound to be tied up with the body language of the speaker. And we are 'broadcasting' our body language to the world at large, virtually all the time. We can't help it: we can't switch off the broadcast:

'Is there anything the matter, dear?' is a response to body language.

'Don't trouble him now. Can't you see he's tired?' is another one.

The *visual* aspect of communication is there all the way through life. Its loss must be one of the most terrible deprivations of blindness.

So what have I been 'broadcasting' all these years? What have *you* been broadcasting? We are responding to the body language of everyone else around us, and they must be responding to ours, so it follows that you and I have been putting out a constant stream of body-language information since the day we were born. Indeed, for our first year or so of life, body language — along with screaming, weeping, and laughing — was the only language we had available to us. We used it before ever we had access to the language of words, and we've been 'speaking' it and 'hearing' it all our lives. Is this, perhaps, why it remains such a potent means of communication? I kept coming back to the blank realisation that I'd hardly given it a thought. And I suppose that's true of most people.

Fashion models think about it, though. So do actors and dancers. Television presenters, chat-show hosts, anchor-persons — anyone in the public eye — *they* all think about it. Some of them actually pay coaches to help them get it right.

Politicians think about it, too. Adolph Hitler thought about it — there are some amazing photographs of Hitler, practising in front of a mirror, trying out different facial expressions. Churchill thought about it. So did Lincoln.

These are all callings, trades and professions, the members of which earn their living by making people *want to pay attention to them*. They are all professionals at making people want to keep paying attention. It's their job to send messages that people are going to want to listen to and remember — and (it is hoped) agree with, and act upon. Strange, isn't it, the way we advocates seem to have been left out of the company?

We qualify. It's our job, as much as any one of theirs, *to send messages that people are going to want to listen to, remember and agree with — and act upon*. That happens to be as good a definition as you are likely to find of what advocacy is all about. Advocates qualify. So why are we the only public performers who aren't members of the body-language awareness club? We are, after all, descendants of an old and colourful profession. We go in for enormous amounts of visual display. A judge dressed in his most formal robes, all scarlet and ermine, full-bottomed wig and buckle-shoes, is as visually impressive as an Admiral in all his finery, or any archbishop. The only ones we can't compete with are the Household Cavalry. And what other profession, than ours, is provided — at public expense — with a perfectly equipped small theatre, along with a completely captive audience, so that we can mount our *own* productions — at the same time as playing the leading role? There's no doubt about it: we advocates qualify for membership of the club that takes those statistics seriously. *Sixty* per cent of the message is conveyed by one's body-language — and no one in the law ever breathed a word to me on the subject.

Why not? Our teachers taught us so much. How did we, as a profession, overlook such an important aspect of our job? It can't be that we are too shy. Suggest to ordinary people that trial advocates are really rather shy, and watch them collapse with laughter. Why is it? Why do we feel uncomfortable at the thought that we have a duty to take this seriously? The question has to be a rhetorical one. I don't know the answer. But this is a reality and constitutes *two thirds* of the language of advocacy.

The Hon. Barbara Gamer, one of San Diego's Superior Court judges, once quipped that in her court 'the attorney who wears polyester has the burden of proof'. Jurors are constantly commenting on the clothes advocates wear: 'He spoiled his professional appearance by wearing a very distracting pink tie with blue polka dots'; 'He was dressed in a sloppy suit, which gave the impression of a disorganised and rather shoddy professional.' They comment on how much moving around there is, on how tidily or otherwise counsel maintains his or her books and papers. They comment on facial expression, hand movements, gestures generally, hair-style. They even comment on the kind of watches advocates wear, and on the kind of pens they use.

These are American comments, of course. Where jury trial still exists throughout the English-speaking world, advocates are not allowed to de-brief their jurors. Nor indeed is de-briefing allowed in all places in America. But in *all* jurisdictions body language still matters. And a whole sub-division of body language relates to what you wear. Some members of the Bar in England think it's all right to go into court with a half-destroyed, disintegrating

wig on their head, with crumpled linen at their throat and a collar
that publicises how often it has been worn. Torn gowns are not
uncommon. But they all detract from the job the advocate is
supposed to be doing.

Every gesture you make, so it appears, makes an impression on
your decision-maker — particularly if you are appearing in front
of a jury. Every change of expression on your face is noted. How
you move your head and how you hold your chin are particularly
powerful 'words' in body language. Looking over your glasses at
the jury is, so it seems, particularly risky because it makes them
feel you may be condescending to them. How you stand is
apparently important; and very important, too, is what you do
with your shoulders.

If this is all so — and it is supported not only by the work of the
psycholgists but by the comments of jurors and other observers
in court as well — then we advocates have a lot of catching up
to do. How should we do it?

In increasing numbers advocates are turning to professional
actors for guidance. There are many seminars on offer, and
people who have attended them usually say they learned a lot —
learned a lot of fairly obvious things they had never focused on
before, but things which, once looked at and understood, made
them feel much easier in court. Whether you decide to investi-
gate this kind of teaching is a matter for you, and no book can
achieve as much as an expert hands-on 'coach'. All I can aspire
to do here is to touch on the main problem areas and make some
admittedly simple suggestions.

First, go and look in the mirror and get used to doing it without
embarrassment.[13] All other public performers take this for
granted. Lock yourself into a room — take a drink with you if
you feel like it — and examine the mirror *until a total stranger
peers back at you.* This shouldn't take longer than a few

---

[13] I will probably be accused of being inconsistent in recommending this, for
in a much earlier book I said that I was *not* suggesting one should go off and
stare into a mirror. In the intervening years I have changed my mind. The mirror,
however intimidating, is an important tool.

moments. You will suddenly come face to face not with the most familiar face in the world, but with someone you hardly recognise. It happens quickly when it happens, like a sauce thickening, and it can be a little unnerving. But this is the 'you' the world sees. This is the unfamiliar person your jurors encounter in court.

Now find the courage to talk to this unfamiliar you. You are completely private and nobody is watching. If you can't think of anything to say, recite a bit of verse. Don't flinch. It's that person you are looking at who's earning your living for you, who's going to perform brilliantly or less than brilliantly. Face the reality that *this* is the person on whom your career depends — as well as the fate of your clients.

Stay with it, and now start looking at a few specific things about that person in the mirror. Take particular note of forehead, brows, eyes and eyelids, the cheeks near the nostrils and the nostrils themselves, and the mouth and chin. These eight bits of the face are the message-senders. Even when you are fast asleep these eight keep on transmitting messages to anyone who's looking, and when you are awake they are beaming out their messages powerfully and without a break.

How mobile is the forehead? Does it corrugate itself into wrinkles as the eyebrows come up? If it does, the message it almost certainly sends, by doing that, is one of surprise or doubt. If, on the other hand, the brows come down and cause vertical furrows to appear over the bridge of the nose, the message is potentially a threatening one. It suggests anger. Indeed, if the mouth turns upward at the same time, the message is potentially one of nothing less than sadism.

Now consider the eyes and the eyelids. How much of the coloured part of the eyes — the iris, the disk — is exposed? With some people, you can see the entire circle of the iris much of the time. The message usually conveyed by this is that the owner of the eyes is wide-awake, alert, tense maybe, startled perhaps — or even fanatical. Bring down some cover from the eyelids, however, reducing the amount that can be seen of the disk of the iris, and the message becomes one of calmness, balance and 'normality'. Bring the eyelids down a little further and the message becomes one of disinterest or, alternatively, deep thought. Lower the eyelids further still, and the message is one of fatigue. If the lids are held high, exposing the whole of the iris, while the brow is pulled down, the message is one of potentially intimidating intensity.

Notice how immediately the face can formulate and send these messages, ringing all kinds of changes with those eight basic transmitters. A few *regular* minutes of detached observation, looking at yourself as objectively as you can, and you will see exactly how they operate. You will also be able to see whether they operate on *your* face in such a way as needs attention.

The most common problem with an advocate's face is the frown. Many people, when they speak, furrow the brow above the bridge of the nose, and although they aren't aware of it, they give the appearance of *difficulty*. And different degrees of frown send different messages — all of them conveying some sense of discomfort to the decision-maker.

The next most common problem are the eyes. Too many of us show our tenseness and intensity by having too much of the disk showing, and this can actually frighten a jury. Just a tiny bit of cover from the eyelids, however, and the message becomes infinitely more comfortable and relaxed.

Look, examine and experiment. Remember, you are *not* making a fool of yourself. Take particular note of mouth and chin. The mouth can convey an enormous amount, and a slightly raised, slightly thrust-forward chin usually conveys defiance, obstinacy, determination and strength. Tilt your head slightly to one side and notice how everything transmitted by the eight message-senders changes somewhat — subtly but unmistakably.

Many people find this all a bit hard to think about, and certainly to do. But remember your duty to yourself, to your success as an advocate and to your client. If two thirds of your message comes from those eight points on your face, from your shoulders, from your hands, from your body generally and from what you wear, it might reasonably be argued that you have an obligation to know what you are transmitting.

We come now to another thing the psychologists have discovered, and another thing they never told us about when we were students: colour. The advertising agencies and the marketing experts have been taking colour seriously for over half a century. They realise that the success or failure of a product-line in a supermarket depends on how it is packaged: the colour and design of the packaging can be decisive. Different colours, so they have discovered, have different subliminal effects on the beholder. The reds, for instance, create an urge for activity. The blues and the greens have a calming tendency. The brighter shades of yellow are, apparently, 'magnetic' and 'attractive'. Crude, primary colours — what we sometimes think of as fairground colours — tend to promote feelings of energy and the need to *do something*. Pastel shades, on the other hand, have the opposite tendency, reducing one's inclination to act decisively.

If all this sounds like the product of fertile minds run riot, consider this: American football teams used to make a point of painting their home-team dressing rooms in 'savage' colours, while the visiting-team dressing rooms were decorated in gentle, pastel, shades. After a while, it was noticed that the home teams seemed to come out onto the field in a mood which was discernibly — and consistently — more aggressive and taut. The pattern became so noticeable and so consistent that reasons were searched for, and when it was discovered that the dressing rooms were totally different in their decor, the differences were eliminated. When that was done the home-team advantage seemed to diminish, and in the football stadiums of America both home-team and visitors' dressing rooms are now painted in the same way — in bright, rather harsh, primary colours.

The average person, and the average lawyer, has very little awareness of such things. What goes on in the human mind is only broadly understood, and most people have a kind of instinct which encourages us to scoff at what we are not familiar with and don't understand. But this business of colour goes much further than the interior decoration of football dressing rooms. It has been discovered, for instance, that every human being's skin tone — irrespective of race — 'leans' either towards a 'blue base' or a 'yellow base'. Unless you have a trained eye, you are unlikely to be able to see for yourself whether any given individual has a blue bias or a yellow bias, but the difference is a very real one and, although we don't know what we are seeing, we are nevertheless influenced by it. Let me explain.

All shades and hues of colour 'lean' towards one or other of those two primary colours — blue or yellow. Every garment in every clothing outlet in the world is made of fabric which is either blue based or yellow based. As a rather crude illustration, consider the difference between a fire-engine red and a red which is more plum-coloured. The first has a leaning towards yellow, and the second a leaning towards blue. Even white material has such a bias — if you compare a blue-based white with a yellow-based white, holding them next to each other, you will probably have no difficulty in seeing the difference.

So, why is this important? *Is* it important, indeed? It certainly seems to be, and for the following reason: if a person with a blue-based skin tone wears yellow-based clothing, that person is likely to look slightly ill. There will be something about this person, something quite indefinable, which makes the beholder feel there is something 'wrong'. Without knowing why, the beholder will be aware that something about this other person makes him feel less than comfortable: 'There was something about her I didn't like. I can't put my finger on it, but she always made me feel a bit uncomfortable.'

This same subliminal discomfort in the beholder is also produced if the wearer 'mixes' colours. If a blue-based person wears clothes some of which are blue-based and some of which are yellow-based, the same subliminal message is transmitted. Again, the decision-makers feel that there is something disquiet-ing about this advocate, without having the first notion of why they feel this way.

And what effect is produced if a person only wears clothes of the 'right' colour? The 'feeling' the observer gets is that this person is vibrant, healthy, energetic and — and this is purely subliminal — magnetic. Above all, the observer feels 'comfortable' with this person — and the advocate who can make his decision-maker feel comfortable in his presence has already taken a huge step in the right direction.

How do you know whether you are wearing the 'right' colours? The ideal way is to seek help from a 'colour consultant', but there's no need to take it that far. When next you go to buy, say, a shirt, hold the garment up under your chin and note the effect. If it is the 'right' colour for you, you are likely to notice that your eyes look a little brighter and that the colour in your cheeks makes you look healthy. If it's the 'wrong' colour, your eyes will seem dull by comparison and you are likely to feel you look a little pasty — or perhaps florid — but noticeably less than completely healthy.

Do the same with suits, and particularly with neckties. This isn't an illusion and it isn't imaginary. If you start looking out for it, in yourself and in other people, you'll find that your eye quite soon becomes 'trained'. When that happens, you will realise how many of us are walking around, broadcasting a message that we are less than we are. It doesn't take much practice to start seeing all this fairly clearly, and it can become quite fascinating to observe the awful mistakes some people are constantly making. Take this as seriously as it deserves to be taken, and don't condemn yourself to starting every case with an indefinable but real disadvantage.

Lastly, in this chapter, we come back to the matter of *voice*.

For several years now I have been asking seminar audiences — virtually all trial advocates of different levels of experience — to let me know, by a show of hands, how many of them have had *any* training in voice-production. The results are consistent, and somewhat dismaying: less than 2.5 per cent of advocates have had any education at all in the use of their voice.

Yet again, it's an illustration of the rather mystifying lack of interest our profession exhibits when it comes to basics. Movement, gesture, facial expression, what we do with our eyes, colour, voice — we are astonishingly ignorant, as a profession, of all these aspects of the language of advocacy. And again, it's probably due to the fact that nobody focused our attention on any of these things while we were students or when we first entered the profession.[14] But to be as ignorant as most of us are about our voices really is unforgiveable — especially since *this* is the vehicle we think conveys the biggest part of the message. One of the worst things an advocate can do in court is to speak in a voice which cannot be comfortably and effortlessly heard and understood; yet in every court building there are advocates who sin against this obvious and basic rule. More comments from jurors: 'Speak up! Don't mumble!', 'He needed speech-therapy', 'Half the time I couldn't hear him.'

The human voice is, above all, a very *interesting* mechanism, and it has *six* operating parts. It is very like an instrument from the woodwind section of the orchestra. Like the oboe and bassoon (and, indeed, the bagpipes) it has a double reed which originates the sound. This double reed is found in the larynx, commonly referred to as the 'Adam's apple' or 'voice-box', and these 'reeds' are known as the 'vocal chords' or 'vocal folds'. They are set vertically in the larynx and they tend to be longer or shorter in different people, depending on the length of neck. The shorter the vocal chords, the higher tends to be the 'pitch' of the sound they produce; and conversely, the longer the chords, the deeper the voice.

You can often see this demonstrated in opera singers. Luciano Pavarotti, for instance, one of the world's finest tenors, seems to have virtually no neck at all; whereas Robert Lloyd, one of the world's most distinguished operatic basses, stands well over six feet tall and has a noticeably longer neck. These 'reeds' in the voice-box, as I say, are what originate the sound of the voice.

Again, like the instruments of the orchestra, the human voice has *resonators*. Resonators are what produce the individual sound of the various instruments. The French Horn, with its convolution

---

[14] It is encouraging to learn that the Bar of New South Wales now offers a voice-production course to new advocates. It is very well spoken of and represents a significant move in the right direction.

of tubing ending in a large 'bell', produces a distinctly different sound from a trumpet: their entire shape, from mouthpiece to bell, constitutes the resonator. Or consider a concert harp and compare it with a guitar. They both rely on an original sound produced by plucked strings, but the *shape* of the box to which those strings are connected — the resonator — is responsible for the very different sounds they make. These resonators are all *hollow* and they convert the original source of the sound into something much bigger and utterly distinctive.

Unlike orchestral instruments, which have only one resonator, the human voice has no fewer than four. Wherever there is anything that might be described as a hollow cavity in the human body, this acts as a resonator for the voice. The mouth is the most obvious example, but the chest is another one. Strike your chest gently with the flat of your hand and you will realise that it behaves very slightly like a drum: you produce a muffled, but distinctly hollow sound. (Physicians tap the chest, and listen to the resonance, so as to diagnose whether, and if so where, there is congestion.)

The third 'hollow cavity' in the human is the upper part of the nose and the sinuses; and the fourth and last is the skull itself. Although it is filled with grey matter, the skull nevertheless has enough 'room' for it to act as a faint resonator for the voice.

The *sixth* constituent part of the voice is the 'bellows' which produces the flow of air through the voice-box. The air in our bodies is largely contained in the lungs, but producing a smooth, controlled, flow of air through the voice-box is the task of a muscle known as the 'diaphragm'. This is an arch-shaped band of muscle which runs from side to side of the body in the region of the navel.

Singers, and others who make a study of voice-production, are taught to take breath into the *lower* part of their lungs rather than, as is the case with most people, the higher part. By filling the bottom part of the lungs first, the arch-shaped diaphragm is pushed downwards into a flattened position. But, since this is not its position in repose, it has a constant tendency to return to the shape of an arch. This tends to push air upwards, out of the lungs and, if the person is speaking or singing, through the voice-box.

Singers refer to the diaphragm, and the assistance it provides in controlling the smooth flow of air, as their 'support'. And a support it really is. If you know how to breathe in this way, and if you learn how to use your diaphragm in the right way, you will find that the whole business of speaking becomes a much less effortful experience. In particular, when you find yourself getting nervous — and it happens to us all — take a breath into the lower part of your lungs and consciously push down your diaphragm. Flex the muscles of your abdomen. For some reason, this will almost certainly increase your 'comfort level' and help reduce your nervousness.

But how, you may ask, do I know when I'm pushing down my diaphragm? It's not difficult. Make a point of breathing in through your nostrils and *consciously* sending the air towards your abdomen rather than towards your shoulders. Make sure your shoulders do not come up and that you don't expand your upper rib-cage as you breathe in. In this way, you will automatically engage the diaphragm and push it into its flat position. And you will find that it's easy to control the flow of air that activates your voice.

Try, now, the experiment of letting your voice resonate *only* in your mouth. You'll catch on quite quickly if you persevere. Then permit your voice to resonate, as well, in your nose. This may sound a bit funny at first, but ease it off slightly and you will find that mouth and nose together produce a brighter, more penetrating sound. Then think about permitting your chest to come into play. It is one of the surprises of experimenting with the four resonators that simply thinking about them *consciously* tends to bring them into operation.

As to the head resonator, this is pretty much a subsidiary one, and for the purposes of speaking — as opposed to singing — don't struggle, trying consciously to bring it into operation. Mouth, chest and nose, however, *are* important, the chest adding a dimension of richness and warmth to any voice. And if ever you find yourself in a courtroom with rather 'dead' acoustics, so that you feel your voice isn't carrying easily, all you have to do is consciously to increase the use of the nasal resonator. This will invariably give your voice a slightly sharper 'cutting edge' and make it carry effortlessly in the most unacoustic of rooms.

Very well. Let's get back now to what lawyers normally think of as the language of advocacy. The next part of this book deals with a host of words and phrases, endlinks and gadgets, that make everything so much easier in court.

PART TWO

WORD AND PHRASES, ENDLINKS AND GADGETS

9   Interchanges with the Bench

Always *begin* with:

- 'May it please your Lordship', or

- 'May it please you, my Lord', or

- 'If it please your Ladyship', or

- 'If it please your Honor',

or any combination of the above.

In America, many advocates say 'May it please *the Court*'. This is perfectly correct, but it wastes an opportunity. It moves in the direction of depersonalisation and away from intimacy. The small theatre that the system puts at our disposal is intimate theatre. Everyone there becomes a character in the drama being played out. If it's good theatre, everyone feels *personally* involved.

Judges sit through many boring, poorly presented cases, and they often have to remind themselves that, as judges, they have a duty to take the rough with the smooth. But if they get a really well-presented case, about something that matters, the human being on the bench finds that he or she gets involved too. And this is what you must be aiming for from the outset. *Everybody* involved in your extremely important small theatre presentation ought to feel a deep personal involvement. 'May it please your Honor . . .' addresses a human: 'May it please the Court . . .' addresses an institution. Decide for yourself which you like better.

One hardly ever hears 'May it please the Court' in Britain, just as no British advocate says 'Your witness!' at the end of an examination. Idiom differs.

When do you begin with those words, 'May it please, etc.'?

- You use them at the very outset, when you first address the judge in the case.

- You use them just before you begin questioning the jury in *voir dire*. (This can't be done in Britain of course. Defending a borderline case of dangerous driving, once, I asked my judge if we might inquire, at jury selection, if the prospective jurors could actually drive a car or not. He refused.)

- You use the words, addressed to the judge, just before you turn to the jury to begin your opening speech; and you use them, again addressed to the judge, just before you start any *other* addressing of the jury.

- If it is you who are to kick-off after the mid-day break, resuming whatever you were doing before the court rose, always start off the new session with a glance at the bench and a low-voiced 'may it please your Honour'. Indeed, this advice applies to *any* resumed hearing after *any* break. Nothing should be re-started by you without a 'may it please . . .'.

Don't wait for the judge to acknowledge this. Some judges will — 'Yes, please carry on Mr Gray' — and if they do, you simply get on with whatever the task is. Some judges don't respond at all. Don't be alarmed by this. Just get on with whatever it is you have to do.

The expression 'If it please your Lordship'/'If it please your Honor', has another use. It is courteous, when the judge has made a ruling of some kind, to *acknowledge* that he has done it. The most useful phrase for acknowledging the judge is 'If it please your Lordship'; and interchangeable with this is 'If your Lordship pleases'. But note: when the American judge rules on your objection — usually with the single word 'sustained', or 'overruled' — this does *not* call for any acknowledgement.

'If it please your Honor' is slightly better as an acknowledgement than 'So be it, your Honor', probably because 'so be it' can sometimes sound a little sullen. 'If it please your Honor' has no such overtones.

Take care with the expression 'Very well, your Honor'. Although it sounds like a perfectly good way of acknowledging your judge's ruling, it has come to be regarded, in America, though not apparently elsewhere, as a potentially *defiant* response, and it makes some judges bristle. If you ever use 'very well, your Honor', take care that your tone of voice doesn't convey any truculence or resentment.

So much for starting and acknowledging. Moving on, are there any guidelines as to how to talk to the judge during the course of the trial? There are indeed. If you are interested in making your advocacy elegant as well as professional, there is one quite simple guideline: *always try to avoid asking the judge a direct question.* This is *not* in any sense an inflexible rule, but if you simply aim for it, and put it into effect whenever you comfortably can, it will bring an agreeable 'polish' to your advocacy. For example:

- *'I don't know if* your Honor has had the opportunity of reading our trial brief?' instead of 'Has your Honor read our trial brief?'

- *'I don't know if* your Ladyship will be rising at the usual time today?' instead of 'Will your Ladyship be rising at the usual time today?'

- '*I wonder if* your Honor would be kind enough to look at page 6 of the contract, clause 17?' instead of 'Would your Honor look at . . .?'

- '*I wonder if* we might have a short break at this point, my Lord? I need etc. . . .' instead of 'Could we have a short break . . .?'

Those phrases, 'I don't know if . . .' and 'I wonder if . . .', are very useful. They should be voiced rather quietly and spoken rather casually, and not in any sense emphasised.

Suppose you have some slightly unusual request during the trial. You'd like, for instance, to have something brought into court, or you'd like to have something re-arranged. A useful phrase is 'I hesitate':

- '*I hesitate to trouble your Honor, but* I wonder if the overhead screen could be moved slightly so that the jury can see it more easily.'

- '*I hesitate to intrude* on m'friend, my Lord, but I feel a point of law arises here which your Lordship may feel needs to be explored.'

There will be many times when you have to lead a judge through a particular document, and many times when you have to take him or her through the meat of a reported case. On such occasions, try to avoid saying 'I refer your Honor to . . .' or 'Referring your Ladyship to . . .'. This can sound as if you have assumed command — and although you should aim to be quietly in command all the way through, you should never show it. Say instead:

- '*I wonder if I could bring your Lordship to* page 123 at letter C. There, as your Lordship will see, the learned judge considered the question of . . .' or

- '*Might I refer your Honor to* page 98 of this witness's deposition? At number 14 through 19 he said . . .'

In this last example you are asking the judge a direct question, but that doesn't matter. You are maintaining utmost courtesy. Here's another perfectly proper question:

- *'May I invite your Ladyship's attention to* clause 9, Roman numeral vii?'

When you and your judge are deep into the examination of a document or a case, you can properly use the following:

- *'Does your Lordship see* the next sentence?'

- *'If I could bring your Honor to* the paragraph at the foot of page 123 . . .'

- *'If I might invite your Ladyship to come to* page 125, second paragraph, . . .'

- *'May I refer your Lordship, now, to* the case of Craddock? It's unreported, I fear, my Lord, but a transcript is available.'

During such an examination of a document or a piece of case law, it is likely that your judge will make comments and/or ask questions. Although what you are aiming for is an easy-going intellectual discussion between two intelligent people, you have to maintain the courtesies throughout. The following phrases are helpful:

- 'I hear what your Honor says. Perhaps I could deal with your Honor's point by putting it this way . . .'

- 'I think I see what's troubling your Honor. It might be helpful if we came immediately to the case of . . .'

- 'I'm grateful for your Lordship's indication. Might I bring your Lordship to . . .'

- 'I take your Ladyship's point. The way I put it is this:'

With *all* these rather antique-sounding phrases, make a point of speaking them as easily and effortlessly as if you normally used them round the dinner-table. Avoid sounding as if you are consciously using 'ceremonial' language. They are easy to learn, but aim from the outset to use them *lightly,* as if this kind of language were the most natural thing in the world. If you over-lard your politeness, it will sound pompous and your judge may be irritated.

In British, Australian and many other courts, one constantly hears the phrases, 'I'm obliged', 'I'm much obliged to your Lordship', 'My Lady, I'm obliged'. They are the barrister's ways of saying 'thank you', and it's part of the idiom to thank and keep thanking the judge for just about everything. It is also a habit of the barrister, quite often, to say 'I'm obliged' when a witness has answered a question — not all the time, but at the end of every half-dozen questions or so.

If you do this in America, you will be regarded with mystification. The expression is never used in the examination of witnesses, and it is hardly ever heard in addressing the judge: 'Your Honor, thank you' or 'Thank you, your Honor' is what one normally hears. Even then, one has to go carefully. The American judge regards himself or herself as someone who is sitting there to make sure that the rules are followed. If he or she is called upon to exercise discretion, it will be exercised in accordance with the rules. The judge doesn't feel that he or she is dispensing favours, and may be slightly discomforted by being thanked overmuch.

If you *have* asked the judge for an indulgence — a late start on the following day, for example, to serve your personal convenience — then 'I'm greatly obliged, your Honor' would be perfectly acceptable; but go easy when you thank the American judge for doing nothing more than his or her judicial duties.

We come now to the problem of interruptions from the bench. Some judges are extremely courteous, pleasant people: some are natural bullies. Some are patient and painstaking, balanced and judicious by nature: some are crude, tetchy and impatient, given to jumping to conclusions. Some are extraordinarily intelligent and some are almost incredibly obtuse. We advocates have to learn to cope with all of them.

One has to keep in mind, all along, the distinction between trial by judge and jury, and trial by judge alone. When there is a jury, it is possible for the advocate to appeal *past* the difficult judge to the lay persons who will ultimately deliver the verdict. If the judge is indeed a bully, the jurors are likely to notice the fact quite quickly, and they may feel sympathy for the advocate's difficulties. When one is handling a case before the judge alone, however, one has to avoid getting on the wrong side of the decision-maker; one has to do one's best to neutralise any unpleasantnesses he or she may have.

In England and most other jurisdictions, virtually all civil trials come before a judge alone. Most of us had our right of trial by jury slowly whittled away during the twentieth century, and if you have a largely civil practice — negligence, personal injury, landlord and tenant, intellectual property etc. — your cases will be heard before judge alone. In America trial by jury is still the norm for almost all civil cases, and although 'bench trials' are not uncommon, they are probably the exception rather than the rule — in most really serious cases, anyway.

Jury advocacy and judge-alone advocacy, obviously, have be slightly different. Where you are facing a judge alone, no matter how impossibly difficult he or she may be, you *must* stay on the right side of him or her.

The difficult judges are usually the less intelligent ones. One of the things they have a problem remembering is the need to be, *and to appear to be*, nothing less than *just*. It takes a fine, focused intelligence to preside over the dispensing of justice. It's a natural human inclination to take sides and to push your own view of things; and sitting there as a judge, putting out an energy which is constantly and reassuringly impartial, requires intelligence and dedication. The more intelligent, aware judges are usually wonderful at it, but there are some judges out there who appear never to think about it; and some judges have difficulty in finding for an advocate who has annoyed or upset them. It's not how things ought to be, but it's an understandable fact of life.

Being fastidiously polite in the presence of a boor isn't easy; but this is what professionalism is all about — doing something expertly — and fastidious politeness is utterly essential when dealing with the difficult judge. As it happens, politeness comes easily when dealing with one of the good judges, so the rule is a very simple one: with both good and bad judges, it is in your interest, and in the interests of your clients, to maintain fastidious politeness and an undiminished attitude of respect. Even if you think your judge is a rude, ill-educated boor, behave towards him or her with perfect courtesy. You'll accomplish nothing if you don't.

If on the other hand, you have a jury sitting there, don't let the judge push you around. Certainly don't let him or her humiliate you by his or her behaviour. Some years ago a very senior barrister was appearing at the Old Bailey in front of London's most notorious bully judge. For a while he put up with the nonsense coming from the bench, maintaining perfect politeness. But eventually he looked the judge in the eye with a cold, level gaze, and said quietly, but very audibly, 'My Lord, I fear that your Lordship is making an already difficult case just a little more difficult'. Then he carried straight on examining his witness. It was an honest rebuke, properly stated, and even that judge got the message.

This is the kind of the thing to which the books are referring when they talk about 'courageous advocacy'. And make no mistake about it: there are times when it takes a lot of courage to stay calm and to persist in trying to make an irascible judge listen to sense — all with utmost politeness. But having some useful phrases at your fingertips is a help.

The judge interrupts: 'What's the relevance of that?' The advocate has a small series of choices:

- 'It will become clear very soon, if your Lordship would be kind enough to bear with me.'

- 'I hope the relevance will become plain during the course of my next few questions, my Lord.'

- 'If your Honour would indulge me a few more questions, I hope to show your Honour the relevance in just a few moments. Does your Honour permit me to continue?'

If one of these doesn't work, and the judge's interruption has come while you are examining a witness, try this:

- 'I'm happy to explain the relevance to your Lordship, but might the witness be invited to leave court while I do?' or

- 'I'm seeking to lay a foundation for later questions, my Lady.'

If the judge interrupts with some such comment as 'That can't be the law', say something like:

- 'I hear what your Lordship says. Indeed, my Lord, I hope to have the opportunity of addressing your Lordship on this very point. If I may continue . . .?'

'I hear what your Lordship says' is a rejoinder that can be used in all sorts of circumstances. It doesn't mean anything, but it serves as an acknowledgement that the judge has spoken, while at the same time indicating that you reserve your position. It's also useful in cross-examination. But since 'I hear what you say' *can* convey an edge of disrespect, use it with care. Don't use these words in any way that might suggest aggressiveness or discontent on your part, no matter how much may be seething inside you.

To end an encounter with the judge — if he or she doesn't end it first — a useful endlink is:

- 'I'm grateful for your Lordship's intervention. Should I resume my examination, my Lord?'

If you have answered the judge's question — if indeed you have had a debate with him or her and you feel he or she has grasped what you were trying to say — you can get back to what you were doing by saying something like:

- 'I hope I've dealt with your Honor's point. Does your Honor wish me to carry on with my questions?'

Starting and stopping often causes the inexperienced advocate a lot of difficulty. We've already dealt with starting, and it's really quite easy. Stopping, elegantly, requires appropriate endlinks.

What is one likely to have to bring to an end, when dealing with the judge? There are only four things (arguably only three): an argument which you are addressing to a judge who is listening but not engaging in much interchange with you; a 'debate' between you and the judge (which is much the same thing); a session of the court; and the examination of a witness.

Let's deal first with ending a session of the court. When an advocate is on his or her feet and the usual time to take the lunch-break (formally known in England as 'the short adjournment) or to end the day comes round, the advocate may wish to suggest calling a halt. In many jurisdictions the phrase used is: 'Would that be a convenient moment, my Lord?' The words '. . . to end this session' or '. . . for your Lordship to rise for the day' are always left unspoken. 'A convenient moment' always means a moment to end the session. In American courts you use the full sentence: 'Would your Honor think this is a convenient moment to break, your Honor?'

As to concluding a submission, an argument to the judge, there is a handful of helpful endlinks I have heard used. Here are some of the nicer ones:

- 'Unless your Lordship has any further questions . . .?' (the words '. . . I'll leave it at that' are left unspoken)

- 'Those are my submissions, my Lord, and I don't think they'll be improved by repetition. Unless your Lordship has any further questions, that's how I put it.'

- 'That's how I put it, my Lord, and I don't think your Lordship will be assisted if I repeat myself.'

- 'Your Lordship's been most patient during my rather full submission, but unless your Lordship would have me deal with any other matter, that's how I leave it.'

You may receive some such answer as 'Well, help me with [so and so]', or 'What do you have to say about [so and so]?', in which case you deal with the point the judge is interested in. Otherwise the judge's response may be something like 'No. Thank you very much, Mr King.'

All these endlinks can be used in an American court, with the substitution of 'your Honor' for 'my Lord'.

From time to time, you are bound to find yourself disagreeing with the judge. There is a time-hallowed way of doing this. Advocates often use some variant of the words:

- 'With respect, your Honour, . . .'

- 'With great respect, my Lord, . . .'

- 'With the greatest of respect, my Lady, . . .'

- 'With the greatest respect, your Honor, . . .'

When you find yourself in disagreement with your judge, do remember that you might be wrong. Don't forget that your judge has a public posture to maintain. *You* can go back to chambers or office: he or she has to stay there. And don't forget that he or she is in ultimate control of the court.

For all the reasons discussed earlier, maintain politeness and niceness, and think consciously about leaving the judge his or her dignity. Take care with your attitude when you say 'with respect . . .', and be willing to 'take the blame' for your judge's disagreement with you, thus:

- 'I hear what your Honor says, but with great respect, your Honor, can that be right? I don't think I put it as clearly to your Honor as I might have done. Will your Honor hear me again, very briefly, on this point?'

- 'I take your Lordship's point, but with the greatest respect, it may assist your Lorship if I put it slightly differently: . . .'

- 'Do forgive me, my Lord. I failed to make the point as clearly as I should have done. What I was trying to advance was . . .'

These three variants communicate your disagreement and provide you with a springboard from which to have another go at convincing the judge.

Many times in court you will hear the phrase 'in my respectful submission . . .'. It's a perfectly good form of words. The only disadvantage is that it has become a bit of a cliché; and cliché should always be avoided if possible. You may care to try using 'the way I put it, your Honor, is this: . . .', which accomplishes the same thing.

We'll deal with the techniques of ending with a witness in the next chapter.

Lastly, get used to the words 'invite' and 'assist':

- 'I would invite your Lordship to consider . . .'

- 'I think it will assist your Ladyship if I . . .'

and, in America, remember one final thing: never say '*Let* the record show . . .'. This, again, suggests that you are taking command. Say instead, '*May* the record show . . .'.

10   Dealing with Witnesses

Let's come back to something we touched on in Chapter 7 on objections — the 'argumentative question'. It's difficult to define satisfactorily, but in broad terms an argumentative question is one which contains a little speech by the questioner as a preamble to the question itself. For example:

'If the collection of the evidence was botched, it cannot be reliable. So tell us, officer, where did you find the glove.'

'Objection. Argumentative.'

'Sustained.'

In England, a preamble like that would be described as 'comment', and it would probably attract the judge's criticism: 'I do hope, Mr Evans, that you are not going to keep on commenting.' — 'My Lord, do forgive me.'

But preambles to questions are sometimes not only permissible, they are important for the smooth flow of an examination. As long as you are careful *not* to try to score points with a mini-speech, a short preamble to your question is not objectionable. Indeed, the great usefulness of a proper preamble is that it enables the advocate to *headline* and *paragraph* his or her examination.

Headlines and paragraphs are things virtually everybody is used to. Newspapers without headlines are unimaginable. Radio news reports use them: the same goes for television. Magazine articles usually have headlines at the start, and 'box' headlines in the text. This is what we are all *used* to.

Since advocacy in court relies upon the spoken rather than the written word, you cannot indicate visually when you are headlining or paragraphing something. But by the use of suitable words and phrases, you can break your examinations (and arguments) into paragraphs as clearly as you could in print. Headlines are as easy to use as they are important. If you don't headline and paragraph whatever it is you are doing, you run the risk of exhausting your decision-maker — in just the same way as you run the risk of wearying your reader if you present him or her with a solid page of print or typescript, unbroken by paragraphs.

In advocacy, paragraphing and headlining are more or less the same thing. You can use any form of words you like, so long as you are alive to the need (a) to let everyone know where you are going, and (b) to make your listeners feel that progress is being made. For example:

- 'Coming, now, to the night of the 18th . . .'

- 'I hear what you say. Can we turn now to . . .?'

- 'Very well. Let's turn to something else. I'd like to ask you about . . .'

- 'I hear what you say, Ms [Witness], and, if I may, I'd like to explore that with you just a little further.' (then, straight into a question)

- 'So be it. Can we now come to the contract itself and look together at clause 3?'

- 'So much for that. Let's move on and come to the morning of the accident itself. You saw something, I believe?'

- 'Thank you for dealing with those matters so openly. May I now invite you to tell us something about the condition of . . .?'

Every time you use such a form of words, you signal to the decision-maker that you have come to the end of something. This always carries the subliminal message that you are that much nearer to the end of your entire task, and you thus achieve a certain *momentum*. If you can hint (and keep hinting) that progress is being made, your listeners are far more likely to keep giving you their unwandering attention. Thus it is useful to employ an occasional link such as:

- 'That's all I have to ask you about that. Let's come now to . . .'

- 'Very well, let's move on. Next, I'd like you to help us with . . .'

- 'Well, I don't want to take up any more of everyone's time on that. Can we turn, now, to . . .'

References to *time*, incidentally, as in this last example, are very useful. Far too many lawyers ignore, or seem to ignore, the fact that both judge and jury have other things to do as well as sitting in court, listening to lawyers and witnesses. Take every reasonable opportunity you have for letting them know you respect their time:

- 'I don't want to take any longer over this than I have to, but could I ask you to deal briefly with . . .'

- 'Well, we must get on. Come now, if you will, to the work-sheets for the week of . . .'

- 'Let's deal with this next matter as briefly as we can, Mr [Witness]. Can you be exact about the date when you first saw Ms Smith?'

I emphasise that you should try to avoid phrases such as 'referring you to . . .' and 'directing your attention to . . .'. They are so obviously 'lawyer-language'. Although most of the examples given in this and other chapters employ all the formality and politenesses needed in court, they can nevertheless be spoken in such a way that they sound as if they are coming from a human being rather than a robotic lawyer. Try hard, all the way through, to sound as little like a lawyer as you can whenever you are not confined by the formalities. Regard any form of 'legalese' as being dangerous to your relationship with the jury.

Indeed, let's divert briefly into this question of sounding, or striving to *avoid* sounding, like a lawyer. Having watched the performance of hundreds of advocates over the years, and having been perpetually curious as to why one is close to genius and another is quite hopeless, I have noticed that the truly successful advocate is the one who manages to suppress his lawyer-ness and replaces it with his human-ness. Such advocates divide their performance into the formal and the informal. When they are dealing with the bench, they use all the appropriate 'antique' courtesies, but, as I mentioned earlier, they do it lightly, as if it were the most natural thing in the world to talk like that. *Whenever* they have the chance to talk in the ordinary language of mortals, however, they sieze it. In particular, when they are talking to jurors, they avoid lawyer-language almost entirely, and use words and phrases which *any* juror might be expected to understand — and relate to.

This really is very important. Make a real point of sounding as little like a lawyer as you possibly can. Work out for yourself a list of words and phrases that, to you, sound like lawyer-language, then struggle to avoid using them during examination of witnesses and in all speeches/statements/arguments to the jury. Indeed, with any court which has lay-people as members — magistrates' courts, courts martial, certain arbitrations — go as easy as you can on lawyer-language. Here is my personal list of words and phrases to be avoided if possible. See how many you can add to it:

Adduce

Analyse

Articulate (used as a verb)

Aspect

Assert

Automobile accident

Aware ('Were you aware
 that . . .?')

Clarify/clarification

Cognisable

Compensatory damages

Concede

Contra-indicate(d)

Contract/contracted (used as
 a verb)

Controversy

Determine ('Did you
 determine that . . .?')

Deem

Directing your attention
 to . . .

Economic loss

Emotional trauma

Elicit

Entitled

Evasive

Evidence (used as a verb)

Evince

Exert

Exhibit (used as a verb)

Extent

Incident

Incur

Indicate ('You indicated
 that . . .')

Inquiry

In relation to

Motor vehicle accident

Parameter

Previous, previously

Precisely

Prior to

Propensity

Purview

Observe

Recapitulate

Refering you to . . .

Reiterate

Review (used as a verb)

Revisit

Solely, solely as a result
 of . . .

Specify, he specified . . .

State, state whether . . .

Subsequent to

Testimony

You testified that . . .

But returning to the language of the examination of witnesses,
let's turn briefly to examination-in-chief, or 'direct examination'
as it is called in America and, sometimes, in Canada. (We'll
come to endings a little later.)

Your objective, in direct or in chief, is to show-case your witness
for the decision-maker, so that he comes across as credible and
reliable. But you also want him — or what he says — to be
interesting. There is bound to be an element of a story in any
witness's evidence. Search for that story and try to build his
testimony around a story-line. We human beings are so 'wired'
that we have difficulty in *not* listening if we think we detect a
story, and if you aim to make every witness you examine into a
story-teller, you will both be listened to in pin-drop silence.

Be very careful with leading questions. Although you are allowed
to lead on some matters when examining your own witness, it's
always better to lead as little as possible. If you need a general
pattern of questioning to guide you through an examination-in-
chief/direct examination, you may find the following helpful:

I think of it as 'the rule of two' and, appropriately, it has two
parts. Let me explain. Although there is no strict requirement in
any of the English-speaking jurisdictions apart from America that
you should 'lay a foundation' for what your witness is going to
say, this business of foundation-laying can be helpful in con-
structing a smooth examination. Get the witness to tell you *how*
she knows it before getting her to tell *what* she knows. Think in
paired concepts:

Q: You said that you were standing at the corner of Caroline
     Street and Derwen Road. I heard you correctly?
A: Yes.
Q: From where you were standing, could you see any traffic
     lights?
A: Yes indeed. The lights for Caroline Street were . . .
Q: Forgive me, Mrs Jones. You can tell us about that in just a
     moment. First I'd like you to tell us: were you able to see
     the traffic lights controlling Caroline Street?
A: Yes, I was.
Q: And *did* you see them as the MGB crossed the junction.
A: Yes.
Q: Very well, tell us what the lights were showing for Caroline
     Street as the MGB crossed the junction.
A: They were red.

Think and keep thinking, 'first *how?* then *what?*'. This is the first part of the 'rule of two'. The second part also involves paired concepts. This time, aim to ask an 'open' question followed by a 'closed' question:

Q: Did you hear anything?
A: Oh, yes.
Q: What, exactly, was it that you heard?

Q: At that point, did you see something?
A: Yes.
Q: Tell us what you saw.

Q: Did something happen then?
A: Yes.
Q: And were you in a position to see what happened?
A: Indeed I was.
Q: Very well, tell us. What was it that happened then?

Apart from anything else, this pairing of open and closed questions adds a little to the story-telling energy of the examination.

During the examination of your own witness, make a point of varying the form of your questions. There are four ways in which you can ask a non-leading question. They are:

(a) The *direct question*: 'What did you see then?'

(b) The *command*: 'Tell us what you saw then.'

(c) The *request*: 'Would you tell us what you saw then?'

(d) The *choice*: 'Which was it? So-and-so or such-and-such?'

If you use only the first form, your examination will sound stilted. If you use all of them it will sound much more like a conversation. Don't try to use one of each in a mechanical rotation: just be conscious of the way that the form of your question can be varied and use the different forms as you feel inclined.

We come now to cross-examination (and remember that in this book we are exploring language rather than technique). There are some 15 or so classic do's and don'ts in cross-examination, but I have dealt with those elsewhere and don't propose repeating myself here. What *does* bear repetition relates to the 'Please answer this yes, or no' type of question.

It's terribly dangerous, demanding a 'yes' or 'no' answer. In England, judges often step in to prohibit it altogether; but even if the judge permits it, it can alienate the jury. This is because it makes the advocate sound like an interrogator, and everybody knows that the answer to such a question is almost bound to be 'yes, but . . .'.

Nevertheless, the yes-or-no answer is a wonderful precision tool; and if used very carefully, it can get by almost every judge and at the same time offer no risk of alienating the jury. Instead of the rather bullying, 'Answer my next question "yes" or "no"', say:

• 'Would you please, *if you possibly can*, answer my next question "yes" or "no"? Did you actually see Bill Sykes in the bar?'

Those words, 'if you possibly can', remove all the sting. Both judge and jury instinctively feel that, of course, it is *possible* to answer with a 'yes' or a 'no', and they tend to look to the witness in the expectation of an answer. And you can go on:

• 'Again, if you possibly can, would you answer my next question "yes" or "no"? Did you etc. . . .?'

The advice which is traditionally given to the cross-examiner is that he or she should use mainly leading questions, and this is advice is sound:

• 'When you heard the noise you have described, you were at the corner of Shaftsbury Avenue and Cambridge Circus. Correct?'

- 'After you witnessed the document, you saw Mr Downing fold it and put it into a long envelope. That's right isn't it?'

- 'When you told him he was being arrested, he said "This is outrageous", didn't he?'

- 'Do you agree that it was raining at the time?'

The cross-examiner is also warned never to ask any question beginning 'Well, why . . .' and 'Well, how . . .', because such questions hand over entirely to the witness. In America, if you ask such a question, you cannot complain that the answer is non-responsive. Virtually anything is responsive to 'Why?' and 'How?'

Another matter of style which it is worth warning you against: some advocates have the irritating habit of saying 'yes' after every answer from the witness. Others constantly say 'I see'. Take care with both of these. Use them occasionally by all means, but don't let them develop into a mannerism.

Headlining/paragraphing in cross-examination calls for no different skills. Paragraphing is exactly the same in any sort of examination. The phrase, 'I hear what you say', is particularly useful in cross-examination, since, probably because of the adverserial nature of cross-examination, it often implies that the questioner doesn't believe a word of it. 'I hear what you say' also acts as a clear ending to a paragraph if followed by some such words as 'Let's turn, now, to . . .'.

Lastly, consider the possible uses of the word, 'help':

- 'Help me if you will, Mr [Witness]. What was the weather like as you came over the brow of the hill?'

- 'Would you help the jury by explaining what you did immediately after that?'

- 'Help us to understand these technicalities, Doctor. What exactly is meant by "an embolism"?'

Very well. Let's now come to a short final chapter on the question of addressing the jury, or any other decision-maker composed of non-lawyers.

Note: I intentionally add this as a postscript because, with less experienced advocates, it is often forgotten. Part of the language of advocacy involves getting *your* witness smoothly into, and then out of, the witness-box/stand/chair.

Calling a witness is easy: 'With your Lordship's leave, I call my first [next] witness, Mr John Brown.' But finishing is sometimes handled clumsily. The accepted way of doing it in most courts is to turn to the judge and say, 'Unless your Lordship has any further questions . . .?', leaving unspoken the words '. . . that's all I want from this witness'. 'No. Thank you, Mr Coni,' says the judge. And then *you* say: 'My Lord, may this witness be released?'

Some jurisdictions have local variations. In Australia and America, one says, 'Your Honour, may this witness be excused?' and in South Africa, 'My Lady, may this witness stand down?'. Check on your local idiom.

The judge will agree. Sometimes he or she will turn to the witness, express the thanks of the court and send him on his way. Sometimes the judge just nods or says something like 'very well', leaving you to deal with it. You do *not* acknowledge this, but simply say to the witness something like, 'Thank you for coming to court. You are free to go now'. And you see one witness safely off before you call the next one. Do *not* suffer the embarrassment of sitting down, at the end of examining your own witness, without getting him dismissed. If you do, you will notice a silence descend upon the court and you'll become aware that things have stopped happening. The longer it takes you to realise that they are all waiting for *you*, the redder your face gets.

11 Arguing Your Case to the Jury

I prepared an opening recently and tried it out on my 16-year-old daughter. I was rather pleased with it. I'd set out the story in such a way that no reasonable person could have come to any conclusion but the one I wanted them to come to. When I finished, my daughter looked at me in silence. Discomfort was written all over her. She didn't say anything:

'Well?' I asked.

She struggled a bit: 'It's great, Dad. Great.'

'Then why aren't you comfortable?'

She thought for a moment: 'You're forcing me, Dad,' she said. 'If I don't agree with you I'm going to feel a fool.' She struggled to find the words. 'You're dominating me. *You've taken away every last scrap of choice.*'

'And you don't like the feeling?'

'Too true I don't!'

One learns from one's children. Always try experiments in advocacy with children. If you have access to an intelligent 11-year-old, always try out your openings on him or her. Advocacy is, in the very last analysis, a form of *teaching*. The best advocacy simply *explains* why there's only one comfortable verdict. It finds a thoroughly honest way in which that verdict could be arrived at, then it guides the decision-maker into greater and greater understanding of why this *is* the comfortable verdict. Teaching and advocacy are very much wrapped up in each other. And if you can satisfy an intelligent child, you stand a good chance with any tribunal you care to name. Children spot weakenesses you don't notice for yourself.

Lisa's discomfort, along with her ability to articulate it, made me understand what I hadn't noticed before: *I had left her no choice.* I had made her *uncomfortable* by taking away her sense that she *had* a choice. She felt put upon. The argument was so neat and tidy, and so reasonably put, that she felt *forced*. If, on the other hand, she had felt *led*, she'd probably have come quietly.

There's a deep principle of advocacy here, I feel sure. In that final speech/final argument, be aware that you want to lead the jurors and not force them. Don't present them with a copper-bottomed, no sensible alternative, *tour de force* of persuasion and irresistible reasoning. Offer them, instead, a way they may care to follow. Get across to the jurors, all the way along, but particularly during your last opportunity of addressing them, that it's for them to decide and your task is to help them as much as you can to a right decision.

Except in America, you may care to consider *not even asking for the verdict you want*. Nudge the jury towards it rather than demanding it of them. You've taught them everything they need to know so as to find for you. *They* know what you want. Remind them of the things you feel are important. Don't leave them with more than two points to consider — three at the outside. Keep it fairly short — all these two-day speeches are quite unnecessary — and have the courage to leave it to them. For some reason, American attorneys shy away from this kind of understatement, perhaps fearing a malpractice suit, but it can sometimes be very effective just to ask for 'the right verdict': 'It's a matter for you, members of the jury.' It's a good form of words, much used in England — particularly by prosecutors — and it builds a strong layer of protection against the risk that the jury will feel you are forcing them.

But you can take it further than that. Instead of just lubricating your presentation with 'it's a matter for you', try to focus on the fact that it *is* a matter for the jurors, and when you say it, mean it. Remember all the way through that what you ought to be doing is helping them through to the verdict they are going to be most comfortable with. No matter how crucial this verdict to you and your career, don't let any frantic energy come off you. You are in the jury's hands, and they are far more likely to go with a leader than give to a beggar. Lead them gently. They are the deciders. They can't be forced. Don't try.

Words and phrases? Anything you like, really, as long as you are kind and remember that you are part of the ceremonial of the court. Here is just a small handful of links and endlinks:

- 'You may feel . . .'

- 'You may well think that . . .'

- 'Can we come, now, to . . .?'

- 'You may well think, members of the jury, . . . [then comes your argument] . . . But it's a matter for you.'

- 'You will remember, I feel sure, what we all heard from the manager of the plant. You recall the way he . . .'

There's a special responsibility on any advocate who is defending in a criminal case. He or she *must* make the jury understand the crucial importance of the burden and the standard of proof. What follows here is only one suggested approach, culled from watching it done and sometimes doing it myself:

There's something I must talk to you about, members of the jury, which affects you, and me, and the learned judge, and everybody in this courtroom. Indeed, it affects everybody in the country, and it's my duty to make sure you don't, somehow, overlook it or treat it as being less important than it is. Before *anybody* can be convicted in this country, you have to feel *sure* that they did it. If you can put your finger on anything to do with the case and say, 'I'm bothered by that', or 'That troubles me', you must go on to ask yourself, 'Am I really sure — or do I feel that there's a reasonable doubt?'. The law doesn't demand that a jury should have *reasons* for feeling there's a reasonable doubt, but juries usually know *why* they feel less than sure. Say, for example, some bystander came up to you later and challenged you: 'How could you possibly have acquitted in that case?' Would you be left standing there, with nothing to say? Or would you find yourself asking: 'How long have you got? Pin back your ears. *These* are the reasons I didn't feel sure.' Let's look together at what those reasons might be. . . .

You heard the witnesses, members of the jury, and you've heard the arguments. It really is, now, what *you* make of it.

Conclusion

There, then, is a survey of the language of advocacy as used in the English-speaking courts of the world. Despite all local variations we have an enormous amount in common, and we probably *all* have something to learn from each other.

In some of our jurisdictions the law is in a sorry state. In England, for instance, over half the population have lost all practical access to the civil side of the law. People turn instead to their political or trade union representatives. British members of Parliament have huge mailbags full of matters that the courts ought to be dealing with. Some people even petition the Queen. In America, where the people still have access to the law and have the *habit* of using the law to stand up for their individual rights, the system is creaking under the pressures of the hopeless and unending conflict known as 'the War against Drugs'.

Because the politicians are in overall charge, and because our populations are, generally, so unaware of what the law is all about, we lawyers, particularly we advocates, have the responsibility to do all we possibly can to save our systems. It's a difficult task, but if *we* don't try, there's virtually no one else who will. The least we can do is to know our job as well as we can know it, to strive for the highest standards in the courtroom, to keep our courage up — and to remember that Justice, in our countries, cannot survive without us.